How I made my first million

Nick Gardner is an award-winning journalist who spent 17 years working on *The Sunday Times* in London where he edited both its 'Money' and 'Motoring' sections. In 1998 he wrote its best-selling book *50 Essential Questions on Money*.

In 2007 he joined the *Sunday Telegraph* in Sydney to set up its 'Personal Finance' section and is now Business Editor of the *Daily Telegraph* and *Sunday Telegraph*.

How I made my first million

26 self-made millionaires reveal the secrets to their success

Nick Gardner

ARENA
ALLEN&UNWIN

First published in 2010

Arena Books, an imprint of
Allen & Unwin
83 Alexander Street
Crows Nest NSW 2065
Australia
Phone: (61 2) 8425 0100
Fax: (61 2) 9906 2218
Email: info@allenandunwin.com
Web: www.allenandunwin.com

Cataloguing-in-Publication details are available from the National Library of Australia
www.librariesaustralia.nla.gov.au

ISBN 978 1 74175 905 1

Set in 14.5/17.5 pt Bembo by Post Pre-press Group, Australia

10 9 8 7 6 5 4 3 2 1

For Grandad

Acknowledgements

Thanks to Alasdair Macleod, managing director of News Limited, for his help and support.

Thanks also to Kiershen Mackenzie, Stuart Austin, Fiona Fraser, Rob Harris and David Rothnie for being such good friends, and also to my brother Jason.

Contents

Preface

In Australia, entrepreneurialism is woven into the fabric of society. Australians aspire not only to home ownership, but to property investment—and they dream of owning not just one property, but an entire portfolio.

Tax breaks on property ownership are turning Australia into a nation of landlords, and that same spirit is fuelling a desire to break free from the nine-to-five culture to a life where their destiny is in their own hands, whether it be through a franchise or a small, independent business. The government fosters such entrepreneurial ambition with generous tax breaks, and while our big banks can sometimes make life difficult for small businesses, many start-ups not only survive, they prosper.

In this book we learn how it can be done, and how others can follow in their footsteps.

An Idea Worth A Million Dollars

Danial Ahchow
Service Central;
established 2005;
100 employees;
$4.7 million turnover

Photo: Anthony Reginato

One day, when Service Central is worth billions of dollars (as I've no doubt it will be) and founder Danial Ahchow is a squillionaire (which he most certainly will be), somebody will say: 'What a simple idea, why didn't I think of that?' So simple, in fact, that the chances are many of us have had a similar idea. But picturing a simple idea and having the determination and vision to make it a reality are two very different things. And simple though Ahchow's idea was, implementing it has consumed the last five years of his life, eaten millions of dollars in investment capital, and only recently made the thirty-two-year-old entrepreneur a millionaire—on paper at least.

But millionaire status is just the beginning. Global domination is also on the company's agenda, and Ahchow has appointed Australian business legend Shaun Bonett, the property developer (and, with a fortune of more than $200 million, a regular on the Young Rich List), and Cliff Rosenberg, former managing director of Yahoo! Australia & NZ, to help steer the company's growth. It is a testament to the potential of the business that both were so keen to get involved. 'I wanted the experience and credibility of these guys and I was so happy they wanted to get on board,' Ahchow says. 'They're easy to get along with and have so much experience, it's been fantastic.'

So what is this amazing idea?

As I said, simple: a quick and easy way for people to find reliable and competitively priced tradesmen instead of flicking through the Yellow Pages in blind faith. 'Looking in Yellow Pages or even scanning online can feel like doing the lottery,' Ahchow says. 'I was trying to find contractors for my dad's cleaning business when I had the idea—there was just no way of telling how good people were or whether they wanted the work.'

Initially, Ahchow thought everything could be automated. 'I had this vision of a black box that could do everything, match all customers with tradesmen, and we'd make millions,' he says, waving arms in the air enthusiastically. 'But since those early days, we've spent about $4 million on IT and we still don't have any little black box. And we probably never will.'

The main reason is that human input is needed to establish who is good and who isn't. A black box just can't give Ahchow the unique selling point that underpins Service Central's business. 'There are review sites for almost everything, but you can't just ask people for reviews of tradesmen. Companies have tried that, and they've had firms giving themselves great reviews, or rubbishing their rival across the road.' Ahchow's vision was of a site that 'had to be independent and be able to prove its independence'.

So Ahchow took on the leg-work himself. Service Central now employs almost 100 people to visit tradesmen and rate them on four indicators. First, they need to be properly registered with their trade association. They also need to be fully qualified and able to prove it. Third, they must have insurance—which happens to be where about 75 per cent of businesses fail Service Central's eligibility test. Finally, Ahchow applies what he refers to as 'the granny test'. 'It's quite subjective, but we ask ourselves: "Would you invite this person over to Gran's for tea?"' Perhaps unsurprisingly, many companies also fall at this final hurdle. 'We don't want to be recommending people who are swearing every other sentence—it's not the image we want to convey.'

The tradesmen are then profiled and sorted by fee ranges and job capabilities: 'We don't want to send a handyman to build a skyscraper, and we don't want to send Multiplex to repair a gate.' Each company selected can register for an annual fee averaging $3000, and a per-job kickback of $7.50 for small tasks and $30 for bigger ones. With more than 3000 businesses now registered, the site's turnover is over $5 million a year and rising fast.

The business didn't really get going until 2005, yet Ahchow made his first million in 2007, when the company was raising capital for further expansion and his 50 per cent stake was valued at $3 million. 'It was weird,' he recalls. But after it happens, 'You don't behave any differently. I still act like I don't have [the money].' Well, almost. 'I've bought a house in Melbourne and a BMW Z4, which is a nice toy. Other than that, I really don't go spending money wildly.'

Ironically, rather than reducing the company's revenues, the global financial crisis helped it become more profitable.

'It resulted in us taking a long hard look at our costs and really cutting back,' Ahchow says. 'We have been reducing staff numbers and radically cutting overheads. Not that it's been forced on us—it's more pre-emptive. The business has continued to grow, but we are preparing for a worst-case scenario. Anything above that is a bonus.'

Ahchow has found more tradesmen applying to get on his books as the crisis has shaken business confidence: 'They want to source as much work as possible, so suddenly we're getting swamped by more and more tradesmen. It was such a struggle at first, but I suppose it's no surprise that in a recession we're getting more applicants.'

In addition to laying off some staff, Ahchow has cut back on some of his marketing costs and focused more on online advertising, which is easier to monitor.

'I use the 80:20 rule a lot,' he says. 'Eighty per cent of your business tends to come from 20 per cent of your customers, so focus on that 20 per cent. Similarly, 80 per cent of your success with marketing will come from 20 per cent of your spend, so concentrate on those elements. It's common sense, really.'

Service Central is getting around 10,000 inquiries a month—and that will jump substantially after Ahchow signs a deal with a national hardware chain to provide tradesmen to its customers. Other big companies also want to get involved: 'We're now speaking to AGL and TruEnergy [about how we can help them] manage their workload to get their [excess] jobs out to tradesmen as well.'

Ahchow says the downturn has also made businesses more open to partnership deals. 'It's a great time to look around to see who you can partner with to strengthen your business.'

To help ensure consistently good service, customers are invited to rate tradesmen when they have finished their work, much as sellers are rated on eBay. If a tradesman falls below three stars out of five, he must explain to Ahchow and his team why he shouldn't be kicked off the register.

Tradesmen may be queuing up to get involved now but in the early days it was a struggle, Ahchow says. 'I had to call 600 plumbers just to get a meeting with one of them, and even then it took four hours to persuade him to pay a modest $80 annual fee to join us. People kept saying they'd heard it all before. It's difficult to keep the faith at times like that, but I had such confidence in the idea—I knew it would work if only we could get enough tradesmen.'

It took a great deal of faith not only for the tradesmen but for Ahchow and his father—who helped finance the project—to stick with the idea. And a slice of luck. 'We advertised on radio. It cost $16,000 a month, which felt like a huge gamble. Then the radio station had a competition where the major sponsor dropped out, so we accidentally became the major sponsor of this Melbourne-wide promotion.' It was the stroke of fortune they needed, he says: 'It got us started.'

'I had to call 600 plumbers just to get a meeting with one of them, and even then it took four hours to persuade him to pay a modest $80 annual fee to join us. People kept saying they'd heard it all before. It's difficult to keep the faith at times like that, but I had such confidence in the idea—I knew it would work if only we could get enough tradesmen.'

The service is now available right up the east coast, from Melbourne through Sydney to

Brisbane, and it's expanding on the Gold Coast. Overseas is next. Ahchow says that while the US does have a similar service, that doesn't mean he can't go there. 'First-mover advantage isn't everything—it depends how you tackle the market. But there is nothing like us in the UK or Europe, and that's a huge market.'

There is still work to do before Service Central dominates Australia. But judging by his success so far, you'd have to say that Ahchow has a very bright future indeed.

Nick Gardner

GOLDEN RULES

1. Keep communicating with your staff. They need to know you're in control and they need to know what is happening. Keep them informed.
2. It's not just about finding smart people, it's about empowering them.
3. Don't promise anything you can't deliver.
4. Use economic downturns to cut costs.
5. Focus on the 20 per cent of your customers who provide most of your business.
6. Never deceive yourself—assume the worst and build your business model accordingly.

Pub Baron Shrugs Off The Worst Of Times

Mark Alexander-Erber
Pubboy;
established 1997;
twelve employees;
undisclosed turnover

Photo: Adam Ward

Mark Alexander-Erber is passionate about things. Things like guns, fast cars, Harley-Davidsons, women and tattoos. He is not, in short, your average millionaire businessman. Indeed, depending which reports you believe about his Pubboy empire, he may not be a millionaire any more. But even if he's not, his wild ride to riches was certainly a colourful one.

Alexander-Erber's language is also colourful—tending to psychedelic.

By his own admission, 2007 (when he turned thirty-seven) was a horrible year. Everything that could go wrong did, including fire, flood, theft and divorce. No ordinary person could have coped with the things that happened to him in '07, he maintains: 'A normal businessman wouldn't have handled it, there's just no f****** way. They would have ended up in a ball in the corner, in the foetal position, sucking their thumb, on f****** medication.

'I got through because I believe I'm the truest essence of an entrepreneur. And that's real. I don't give a f*** what anyone says, that's real. I'm real. You cut me, I bleed. Tell me something funny, I laugh. I see something sad, I cry. It's not a f****** show, this is me.

'People don't see that. They see what they want to see.'

I first met Alexander-Erber in his Paddington, Sydney, offices a couple of years ago, when Pubboy was on the rampage, with a chain of twenty-six hotels pouring their profits into its owner's denim pockets.

The walls of his lavish home—complete with pool table, motorcycles, pinball machines, super-sized stereo and silly-sized TV and computer screens—were covered with framed articles boasting of his business acumen and his inclusion in *BRW*'s Young Rich List. To describe him as media friendly would have been like calling Kevin Rudd slightly smug. It's fair to say that he lost a little of his enthusiasm for the press after his relationship with Amber Petty (bridesmaid to Princess Mary of Denmark) became public. A photo of the two at a Pubboy Christmas party, along with an assortment of bikies including Bandidos chief Rodney 'Hooks' Monk (who was later murdered), stirred a media frenzy very different from the kind he'd been used to.

Alexander-Erber gives his bald head a rueful shake and points out that he's never been a member of a bikie gang himself. 'People try and link me to that; it's a media-driven thing,' he says. As the thinking goes, 'I've got tattoos, a goatee and a bald head, and I ride Harleys, so I must be bad, or I must think bad. It's not like that at all. The Israeli ambassador to Australia is a very good friend of mine. He's a magnificent person, but if I hang around with him people don't suddenly say I'm pro-Israel.'

'On the other hand, I will say I would have some of the bikies I know over to my house before I'd have half the bankers. They're a lot nicer people, and they're real.'

It's unlikely Alexander-Erber has had any of his recent clippings framed for his wall. Those news items carried headlines proclaiming that his empire had collapsed and he was $20 million in debt. It's a subject he'd rather not discuss in detail. But he will admit that at least some of his pubs are in the hands of receivers, reportedly appointed by ANZ Bank, which is said to be owed $10.5 million. 'In 2007, we had a series of events—fires [the Lawson pub in Mudgee], floods [which trashed three of his Newcastle pubs] and robberies,' he says. 'It was biblical. At one point I looked out the window expecting to see a plague of locusts.

'It was biblical. At one point I looked out the window expecting to see a plague of locusts.'

'Then my marriage broke down, which was tough. I had a series of things that forced me to restructure. What I'd like to say is that all the reports that have come out about me have been absolute bull****. We haven't gone bust at all.

'I've restructured. I made a decision to work with the banks. We didn't go bust for $20 million; I'm working with administrators and receivers to restructure the group. Some will be sold to pay off the bank debt. I'm hoping to do some kind of deal to get some of the pubs back and keep moving forward and fixing up all creditors.'

To most people that sounds like an unmitigated nightmare, yet Alexander-Erber says he's 'so happy and so excited' about what's happened he can barely put his feelings into words. 'All this has made me refocus and look at my life and what I want. It gets to the point where you think: "How many cars do you want? How many flash houses do you want to live in?" I've always been spiritual, but I got lost along the way. Now I'm finding I've got time to sit and reflect on where I went wrong.'

What would tip some people into depression or worse is to him a valuable life lesson: 'I don't look at anything as going wrong; I look at it as an experience. I've definitely been let down by people who worked closely with me, and I take responsibility for that. I trusted them too much. I thought they knew what they were doing, and they didn't. It's been an amazing experience, and anyone who counts me out would be foolish.'

Alexander-Erber's eye is still on the future, but it's a calmer, saner future: 'The way I'm going to set things up is going to set me up for the rest of my life. I'm meeting some incredible, spiritual people who are supporting me. I'm excited about that. I'm very fortunate to be learning this lesson at an early age. And I'm certainly not on the bones of my arse.'

Although his flamboyant tattoos—'Live life your own way' covers his back—suggest he crawled up off the mean streets, Alexander-Erber grew up in Vaucluse and was schooled at Sydney Grammar and Cranbrook, where one of his classmates was James Packer. However, he didn't enjoy 'the confines of school' and left halfway through Year 12 to attend catering college.

In 1985 he took a job at the Regent Hotel in George Street. He stayed there until 1997, when he bought his first pub, the Iron Duke. His Pubboy empire grew and grew until he hit millionaire status 'on paper' in 2003. But if that came as a surprise to some, for him it was merely the culmination of a lifetime of entrepreneurial effort. 'My whole life I was making money: washing cars at weekends, doing up cars, various things,' he says.

'From very early, I trained my mind with affirmations and visualisations. When I was fifteen, I'd get up every morning saying: "I am a multimillionaire, I drive a Rolls and I live in a waterfront house." Although those things weren't in my life yet, I trained my mind to think like that and to believe that. Once you believe it, it manifests itself and it happens.'

When the multimillionaire visualisations became reality he thought it was important to reward himself, and he did. 'I've always had two cars, right from when I learned to drive, whether it was a Mustang and a Land Cruiser, or a Porsche and a vintage car. At one stage I had thirteen cars. I don't spend a lot on clothes, but I like guns. I collect guns; I've got about ten pistols. I've got a massive collection of rock 'n' roll memorabilia. I suppose I've spent money on things like that. I've got a tile from the pool that Brian Jones [the founding Rolling Stones member] drowned in. That's pretty cool.'

He regrets that as the Pubboy brand developed his personal life became public property, but the experience didn't frighten him all that much. Indeed, he's now working on a reality-television show about himself that he says Foxtel and one of the big networks have shown interest in. 'It's an excellent capture of my life,' he says. 'I'm very passionate about everything I do. I'm passionate about my children. I'm passionate about my business. I'm single, so I'm passionate about women.

'Money comes and goes. You don't take it with you when you go; all you take is a good soul.'

STEPHEN CORBY

GOLDEN RULES

1. Live your life your own way.
2. Stay true to your dream.
3. Believe in yourself.
4. Make love, not war.
5. Get your priorities straight.
6. And remember who the real boss is—Bruce Springsteen.

An Ad For The Good Life

Grant Allaway

AD2ONE;

established 1999;

fifty employees;

$30 million annual turnover

Photo: Anthony Reginato

Being rich suits Grant Allaway. It's not just that he's young and handsome and has a fortune at his fingertips. Or that he spends obscene amounts of money on handmade shirts and suits. He simply couldn't exist any other way. 'I'd be terrible at being poor,' he admits. 'I'd go mad if I had to think about spending money; if I had to budget or think twice before going out for an expensive meal, or booking a holiday. Those things would really irritate me.'

Just as well, then, that Allaway is boss of AD2ONE, an online advertising agency he has taken from a four-man operation about to go bust in 2000 to a multinational business that turned over $20 million in 2008/09. It has offices in London and Sydney and, after becoming AOL's new online advertising agency, is now the largest such agency in Australia.

As Allaway points out, the 2009 economic downturn was the first where there was a viable advertising alternative to TV, radio and newspapers. In previous deep recessions, online ads didn't exist.

And it's an alternative advertisers clearly like, with revenues 15 per cent higher in 2008 than a year before. Allaway concedes that even so, his UK business would have had a 'relatively flat' year in 2008 had he not won quite a major client—eBay. As a result of its business, however, his revenues zoomed 200 per cent.

'We're having a great recession,' he says. 'We are lucky to be in a sector that is not too badly affected. [That's mostly] because online advertising is relatively cheap, transparent and easy to monitor. Advertisers are leaving other forms of media and [doing their] spending online.'

I meet Allaway at the $12 million waterfront mansion at McMahons Point that he's rented for his stay—after spending £20,000 on first-class flights from London for himself, his wife, Sarah, and their three children, all under five years old. 'Ah, the kids can play up on the plane sometimes, and the other passengers must hate me, but I don't care,' he says. 'The [expense] is worth it because the kids can run around and they get looked after. It's fantastic. I always travel first class now.'

When I arrive the scene is a perfect picture of happy family life, with Allaway's two giggling daughters climbing on his back as he crawls across the floor.

But his life has not always been so idyllic. Born in London, he had a happy early childhood—his father was a financial director for a steel company and his mother was a housewife. 'It was the classic suburban family, 2.2 kids, comfortable existence,' he says. 'I always got the bike I wanted at Christmas and all that. I was particularly close to my mum—a bit of a mummy's boy really. But one morning, when I was twelve years old, my mum didn't wake me up for breakfast like she usually did. It was my uncle instead. I went downstairs and my relatives were all there, and they told me straight: Mum and Dad had been killed in a car crash.

'Obviously I cried and I was shattered, but I didn't shut down. You find a way of carrying on. You just do, even when you're twelve.'

A couple of years later, doctors blamed a painful skin rash on the stress and depression that Allaway suffered in the wake of his parents' death. One thing he didn't have to worry about was money. He received an extra £65 a week in benefits because of his orphan status. 'In 1985, when you were twelve years old with no outgoings, that was a fortune! I had all the latest gear, [running shoes] and tracksuits. And I knew there was a £200,000 trust fund that would kick in when I was eighteen, so actually I never had to worry about money. It's always been there. I've been skint because I've spent it too quickly, but there's always been more around the corner.'

Allaway enjoyed school, where he stood out as the best-dressed student, and by the time he went to university he'd received the £200,000. 'I spent the lot,' he says. 'By the time I finished university at twenty-one, it had all gone.'

He did, however, do one constructive thing with the cash—he put £3000 down as a deposit on a £30,000 flat in Brighton that today is worth about £170,000 ($370,000). 'If that flat—which is a s***hole—can grow in value to £200,000, then I'll have made it all back! That would be something.'

After university, facing poverty for the first time, he found a job with a photography company, cold-calling people to try and sell them vouchers for a family portrait. 'I really took to it,' he says. 'I thought to myself, I'm going to get a job in media sales after this, so I ended up in sales jobs on a variety of magazines, including one that provided a company car, which I thought was the ultimate achievement!' Next he joined the publishing firm Reed Elsevier, selling ad space to corporate clients, honing his sales skills as he worked across its range of publications. Then, in 1995, when the Internet was still in its infancy, he got his first online job, selling online ads for Reed. 'I was having to explain what a website was to all the potential clients,' he says. 'People just didn't understand, let alone want to spend money advertising on it. I don't think I sold anything for a year.'

In 1999 Allaway left Reed and joined a former colleague and friend who was running AD2ONE in London. The agency had been set up to sell ads across a range of websites for Vivendi, a French media company. But after a rapid expansion, the dotcom bubble had burst and AD2ONE was left hanging. 'Vivendi had an AD2ONE office in every major city in Europe.

It closed them all down except [the one in] London because although we were losing money, we did at least have some turnover,' he says. 'Then a small private company came and took over and did nothing, so eventually my business partner Julian and I, who were running AD2ONE at that point, said to the owner: "Look, if we leave, you've got no company. Why don't you just let us take it off your hands?"

'So we did. All we had to do was take on the £150,000 of debt, and the company was ours.'

The pair immediately set about selling across the Vivendi sites and acquiring new sites to sell ads onto. They had a powerful incentive to choose well, he recalls: 'We were only as good as the websites we represented because nobody would want to advertise on rubbish sites. Very quickly we won Disney, Discovery Channel and Eurosport, and started selling ad space to companies such as Ford—companies that aren't interested in response rates, they just want a brand presence on other reputable brands' websites. That's what we specialise in: brand advertising, putting the right ads with the right sites. In Australia we won Lonely Planet and Expedia.com.au soon after opening, which was great.'

His first million came in 2005, when the London company made a clear $3 million profit, which he and his partner split down the middle. AD2ONE started in Australia the same year, selling ads on UK sites visible only to Australian users—mainly newspaper sites such as *The Times* and *The Guardian*, and Sky Sports. It is expanding rapidly and is now the largest online agency in Australia.

> But as he puts it: 'I've always thought I had all my bad luck all at once, back on that morning when I was twelve.

It's all looking up for Allaway now, and some might argue he's had a pretty easy run of it. But as he puts it: 'I've always thought I had all my bad luck all at once, back on that morning when I was twelve.'

NICK GARDNER

GOLDEN RULES

1. Never spend more than you have coming in.
2. Surround yourself with good professionals such as lawyers and accountants to give good advice.
3. Use downturns as opportunities to cut costs.
4. Never forget what makes your business unique.
5. Never underestimate your competitors. Paranoia can be good.
6. Always be home to run the bath for the kids.

Making Millions For Others

Photo: Ella Pellegrini

Charles Anstis
Mandala Financial Group;
established 2009;
five employees;
$750,000 turnover
GPA Matrix;
established 1973;
thirteen employees:
$3 million-plus turnover

He spends four hours a week meditating, treks in the Himalayas for a month each year and has built a dressage arena at his multimillion-dollar home in the Hunter Valley. Charles Anstis isn't your average financial planner.

More concerned with the teachings of the Indian spiritual guru Amma than with his next commission payment, he finds no conflict in the fact that his clients are predominantly money-obsessed, single-minded corporate high fliers or sports stars. Many have no interest in anything beyond amassing a fortune—and Anstis helps them do it. 'Yes, we've got $200 million of clients' money invested,' he says. 'And we've made a lot of people a lot of money—and I'm proud of that.'

But his spiritual bent means he's not content simply to sell his clients the right life-insurance policy: 'My job is as much about counselling my clients as giving them financial advice. Very often, I find myself talking to clients who have more money than they could ever spend, and the money my investments make them each year is immaterial to them.

'So I find myself asking them questions, probing to find out what they actually want out of life. Why are they trying to build their wealth? What do they want to do with their money? You would be amazed at the number of people who have no idea what they're working for, what their ultimate goals are. I help them identify these things and build sensible financial plans to achieve them.'

The process can be emotionally challenging, Anstis says. 'Many people have never been asked these questions before. And aside from that, answering them requires thinking about your feelings, about yourself and your family, in ways that you may never have considered before. The way you structure your estate for inheritance or tax purposes can reveal much more than you think about how you feel about your family and what your values are. Sometimes it's a draining process, and I certainly feel that I'm being trusted with very personal information.'

Anstis, from England's picturesque New Forest, dropped out of Oxford Polytechnic after only a year studying accounting and finance and embarked on a career at Grindlays Private Bank. He was placed in the Middle East department, which turned out to be an eventful secondment. 'We looked after a lot of eminent dignitaries and members of various royal families in the region. They used to come to the south of France every year, so Grindlays

> 'The way you structure your estate for inheritance or tax purposes can reveal much more than you think about how you feel about your family and what your values are. Sometimes it's a draining process, and I certainly feel that I'm being trusted with very personal information.'

sent me down to Cannes to look after them. Most of my work was straightforward banking stuff, but then I started helping them with everything from shopping to arranging their car from the airport. That taught me about service and how you can really add value.'

The ways of Middle Eastern princelings didn't always sit well with those of France. One day in the late 1980s, Anstis says, a member of the Saudi royal family walked into a tiny bank branch in Monaco and said he wanted $US50,000 in cash for a visit to the casino. 'Of course, the French thought this was out of the question and said it would normally take a week, not an hour—not to mention that they didn't know who he was. They asked him for ID, but he didn't have a passport with him. So he went outside to his car, came back with an envelope and pointed to the stamp, which had his head on it! Eventually, after much fuss, they gave him the money.'

During his time at Grindlays, Anstis was posted to Australia on a few occasions. He decided it offered a better quality of life than the dirty streets and grey skies of London. 'My wife and I loved the Hunter Valley, so that's where we headed,' he says. 'I had a bit of money, but not much. But I did have a good contact at Lloyds of London, the insurer, who I knew I could place some high-risk and unusual insurance with—the sort many people wouldn't know where to find.'

Anstis opened the phone book and began cold-calling companies, offering his services. 'Essentially, I would find rare, bespoke insurance cover—often multimillion-dollar policies—to cover footballers or rugby league players that other people just can't negotiate insurance for.' Take a rugby league player looking for injury cover: 'A typical contract might detail wages of $300,000 a year, so that's $900,000 over a three-year contract period. Generally speaking, if a player is injured in Year 1, he might get the current season's pay and that's it. We'll find that player a policy that, in the event of a career-ending injury, will pay out $600,000, covering Years 2 and 3 of the contract as well.'

The sums involved can get very large indeed, Anstis says. When soccer stars play in international matches, for example, 'Their club needs to be covered against the player's suffering a career-ending injury while playing for his country overseas. These policies can be worth tens of millions of dollars, even more than $100 million.'

The work was lucrative, and Anstis's business grew through the 1990s. He was well on his way to his first million. Then he got divorced. 'It's like snakes and ladders,' he says. 'That knocked me back a very long way.'

But he kept on working, and the business kept growing. Eventually, in 2004, Anstis bought GPA Matrix, a financial planning business that he and his partner built into one of Australia's most successful. 'We have tripled the number of clients, doubled the funds under management and tripled the company's value,' he says. 'We now have 3000 clients who pay, I guess, an average of about $2000 a year in fees. I suppose it was around 2004 that I made my first million, but it's not something that sounds an alarm when you pass the landmark. It just creeps up on you.'

So did the stress. About three years ago, someone remarked to Anstis, 'I don't know why you're so stressed, given the amount of money you earn.' Anstis instantly knew the man was right. 'I'd never really stopped to think about it,' he says.

'In that way, I'm guilty of exactly the same thing as my clients—possibly working too hard and not examining all my options properly. But I love what I do, and the moment I stop enjoying it I'll stop doing it.'

In 2009 Anstis decided to go it alone. He set up Mandala Financial Group, taking all his clients—and his tried-and-true business model—with him. He charges an annual fee of 0.5 per cent of the funds he manages, and usually nothing up front.

Because what he earns is a percentage of his clients' wealth, he says, the financial crisis hit him hard. The turbulence in the markets has also meant a lot of clients want constant reassurance and hand-holding. Many also need advice about how to cope with redundancy or shorter working weeks, stuttering cash flows, and the sense that their wealth is vulnerable.

Worried people can be hard to persuade, Anstis says: 'Very often their emotions go one way and the right decision actually lies in the opposite direction. Some people suddenly want to sell into cash, for example, when you know the right move is to ride it out or even invest more.'

Before he set up Mandala Anstis was busy managing the downturn at Matrix, where he spent a lot of time analysing the business on a 'zero-cost accounting basis'. He explains: 'I'd question whether we really needed various products and services at all. I cut back on marketing and PR.' He also thought twice about buying new equipment. 'I began to ask whether the photocopier would last another twelve months. It's a matter of taking a close look at expenses in every area of operations.'

Anstis is still wealthy—and still enjoying his wealth. He may not drive flash cars or own a boat, but he does have a stud farm for dressage horses on his 20-hectare Hunter Valley estate. 'It's a real passion,' he says. 'Although it's a money-making business, I regard it as a hobby first and foremost. The horses are worth about $30,000 each, and it's a highly specialised market. My wife is a wonderful dressage rider—I'm not much good at all.'

Anstis also has five children in private education, 'a considerable expense', although he says he's 'happy when they're happy'. Overall, he says, 'I regard myself as very lucky, and try not to be seduced by money or the trappings of success. I love my family and my home and the freedom I have to travel—something many of my clients hanker after.'

He urges them to follow their heart, not just the money. 'I was recently talking to a client whose lifetime ambition was to buy a motorbike and ride around Italy. I demonstrated to her that not only could she afford to do it now, she could come back in a year or two and be earning more than she was today. She couldn't believe it, but it shows the value of educating yourself or finding somebody who can. Otherwise, you don't know what you might be missing.'

NICK GARDNER

GOLDEN RULES

1. When fear is the problem, activity is the answer.
2. Believe in yourself: you have the ability to change your own future.
3. Play to your strengths: acknowledge your weaknesses and delegate them to someone who is good at them.
4. Stick to your core business and really ensure you are delivering what you promise.
5. Customers are not dependent on us. We are dependent on them.
6. Plan ahead for your outgoings so you are not hit by surprise bills that can cripple you.

The Power Of Flowers

Jonathan Barouch

Fastflowers.com;

established 1999;
thirty-five employees;
$5 million-plus turnover

Photo: Anthony Reginato

For Jonathan Barouch, chief executive of Australia's leading online florist, life really is a bed of roses.

Unlike other young businessmen, he has never had trouble getting financial backing for his company. On the contrary, he's in the enviable position of constantly turning down huge stacks of cash. 'I'm getting offers all the time from private equity companies and other big florists for Fastflowers.com,' he says. 'They've offered me millions of dollars to take me over or for a stake in the company, but I haven't had any offer I couldn't refuse—not yet, anyway.'

Barouch has, in fact, spent much of his young life turning down vast sums of money. He had barely set up the company, as an eighteen-year-old, before the Internet boom had companies queuing at his bedroom door. They offered him 'many, many millions of dollars', he says. 'Silly money—more than the company would ever be worth! But I didn't know what to do with it. And I didn't want the responsibility of having big stakeholders and other people on the board, so I turned them all down and carried on running the business on a shoestring, from my parents' house.'

> 'They've offered me millions of dollars to take me over or for a stake in the company, but I haven't had any offer I couldn't refuse—not yet, anyway.'

It was an extraordinary decision for an eighteen-year-old—especially one who suffers from hayfever and can't stand to be near flowers: 'I've got a sackful of Claratyne in my drawers!'

But Barouch figured he had nothing to lose. 'I didn't take on any debt to start the business, so the worst that could happen was that it would fail and I'd have to do something else. Big deal. Most businessmen have families and mortgages to worry about. I was very lucky.'

This determined entrepreneurial streak is a quality that runs deep in the Barouch family. Jonathan's grandfather was one of the first big furniture manufacturers in Australia, selling his products to the likes of Harvey Norman, David Jones and Grace Brothers. His father was also a businessman, a pharmacist who ran several stores. They and his mother, a freelance journalist, all gave him a strong sense of the importance of financial independence.

The idea for Fastflowers came out of an embarrassing experience in a florist's shop. 'I wanted to buy some flowers for a girlfriend and found it excruciating. I didn't know what to buy or how much money was appropriate to spend. I felt so ridiculous. I thought there must be a better way.'

Searching on the relatively new Internet, he found little competition. 'I found websites in Europe and the US, but nobody in Australia. So I started asking various florists to do our deliveries—since they already had the stock—in return for a small commission for passing on the business to them. The first few turned me down flat—they just didn't get it. But after five or six refusals somebody agreed.'

With savings he had amassed from selling lollipops in the school playground when he was fourteen—'I made a small fortune from that until the headmaster intervened'—and money squirrelled away from odd jobs and birthday presents, he commissioned a company to build a website and business started briskly. There was just a small catch—Barouch was still at school. 'I would dash out of class pretending to go to the toilet, but actually I'd be taking orders from customers or arranging business meetings.'

The teenager soon got a very grown-up break. A newspaper item about him was spotted by the business journalist Paul Clitheroe, former *Sunday Telegraph* columnist and at the time a presenter on TV's *The Money Show*. 'I was at a school swimming carnival when he rang. He was quite famous and at first I didn't believe it was him. I was saying, "Sure, sure," like it was a joke, but eventually he convinced me and I felt like a bit of a goose.'

A crew from the show filmed Barouch working, going to school and doing business on his mobile phone, then taking more orders at home. It might have been a novelty segment, but it did the trick for Fastflowers. Within half an hour of the program finishing, the six-month-old website had clocked up 300,000 hits.

Suddenly, Australia's biggest companies wanted a piece of the young flower magnate. Westpac Bank made Barouch the preferred florist on its credit-card rewards program, giving Fastflowers access to over two million card holders. Then Telstra BigPond also took Fastflowers on as its partner florist. 'That gave us exposure to another two million Internet users. Overnight we became a household brand.'

It was during that time that Barouch realised he had made his first million. Just as important, he knew 'the company was going to be an enduring business. It was a wonderful feeling.'

Today, Fastflowers has a multimillion-dollar turnover and is the only Internet-based florist to own its own stores in Sydney, Melbourne and Brisbane, along with a twenty-four-hour call centre and a warehouse. Remarkably, most of this growth was achieved while Barouch was still studying.

After completing a Bachelor of Commerce degree, he took Honours in Economics and did a Masters degree in Political Science. 'I would study at night and at weekends while all my mates were going to the pub and playing pool, and then I would go back to work and stay at the office till midnight. I did that for about six or seven years. I only finished studying about eighteen months ago.'

Little surprise, then, that Barouch didn't exactly go wild when he hit the million-dollar mark: 'I just concentrated on taking the business forward—planned another marketing campaign. The money is nice. It's given me financial freedom and I've been able to buy an apartment, which is ridiculously expensive in Sydney, and drive a BMW. But it's the other things that give me pleasure. Driving past one of my shops or hearing one of my ads on the radio, that's what makes me feel really good. Like I've built something that will last.'

Barouch now mixes in exclusive circles and provides the flowers for some of Australia's most high-profile events. Dealing with prominent companies such as Ford and individuals such as Al Gore means discretion is a must, so he enforces a strict privacy policy among his staff. 'We have had very famous people call up and order flowers for their mistresses. But flower companies around the world have been sued for leaking that kind of information.'

Barouch recently got married, and his success enabled him to give his fiancée, Amy, the perfect wedding. He hired Sydney Town Hall and had it decorated with more than 10,000 roses and

10,000 tulips. It took fifteen florists three days to assemble the displays. But there were no tears on the day: he was dosed up on Claratyne the whole time.

Nick Gardner

GOLDEN RULES

1. Don't spend more than you have. Keep your budget tight.
2. Don't believe the naysayers. If you have an idea, have enough confidence to see it through—and believe in yourself.
3. Network like crazy. You never know when you're going to make that connection that can make your business explode.
4. Don't be afraid to employ people who are at least as smart as you.
5. Invest in the business—don't blow money on a Porsche if you might need that money to keep the business going.

An Ideal Business Model

Photo: Sarah Rhodes

Shelley Barrett

ModelCo;

established 2002;
forty-three employees (including retail employees at David Jones);
$15 million-plus turnover

It's hard work creating a brand cult that counts celebrities like Victoria Beckham, Keira Knightley, Mischa Barton and Cameron Diaz as devotees. It's even harder to attract such people's attention for free. But that is what Shelley Barrett's beauty company ModelCo has managed to pull off in just seven years.

The company's 125 products are sold in 1000 department stores worldwide—and the financial crisis hasn't held up its growth in the slightest. The stores include *très chic* boutique Colette in Paris, beauty mecca Space NK in London, and lingerie chain Victoria's Secret in the US. In Australia, where it all began, ModelCo has an exclusive concept-store agreement with David Jones.

In 2008 Barrett, aged thirty-six, had the ultimate endorsement when Victoria Beckham was snapped in LA checking her face with a ModelCo eyebrow compact that perfectly matched her pink outfit. Barrett was naturally delighted when her marketing director showed her the picture, which adorned a newspaper's front page, not least because she and the former Spice Girl share a love of pink and handbags. 'I didn't have any idea she used our products until the picture came out,' she recalls. 'We were so flattered. The power of celebrity is huge.'

The only celebrity with whom Barrett has made a formal alliance is Elle Macpherson, who in 2006 became the face of her product Erase Those Fine Lines. The supermodel launched the product at a glamorous event in Sydney, where few fine lines etched the faces of the assembled beauty editors. Elle said she liked the treatment because it offered women a 'non-invasive choice' and that she 'finds the company and Shelley Barrett very interesting'.

Barrett began her business career at twenty-one by launching her own modelling agency. A decade later, it had 1200 models and actors on its books. 'My mother did my accounts and she still has our first cheque for $120,' Barrett says proudly.

Working with models and hair and make-up artists at fashion shows and shoots, she watched sympathetically when the girls winced as they curled their lashes and moaned that they wished there was some other way to create luscious eyelashes. By 2002, Barrett had found one: a heated lash curler that created the desired effect gently, like a hair curling wand. The trick was to find someone to manufacture it.

Fortuitously, her husband Damien was starting an import business at the time. He helped Barrett find a company in Korea that could make the wand and ship it back to Australia. They named it the ModelCo Lash Wand Heated Eyelash Curler and packaged it in pink simply because that was Barrett's favourite hue. 'It became the fastest-selling product in Myer,' she says. Shocked and thrilled by the demand, the couple continued producing the bestseller. ModelCo overtook the model business, and within two years making millions was Barrett's sole focus.

If she needed any reassurance that she'd succeeded, Japan was it. When the company launched there, sales reached $1 million in two months. 'When I started I had no global aspirations,' she admits. 'It was more of a pet project. We grew so quickly, it was sell, sell, sell, and all this money was coming through the door. But then it became about knowing how to spend it wisely. We didn't make huge mistakes, but we could have done things a little better, smarter and quicker if we'd had better systems in place.'

Barrett created a point of difference in a crowded market by creating a slew of innovative dual-purpose and 'quick fix' products—all in her signature hot pink packaging. The first self-administered spray tan (tan in a can) was followed by Liplights, a range of lip glosses that had a mirror and a light for a touch-up in nightclub darkness or the back of a taxi.

“When I started I had no global aspirations. It was more of a pet project. We grew so quickly, it was sell, sell, sell, and all this money was coming through the door.”

And the pace hasn't slowed. Barrett has also launched Fibrelash, a revolutionary eyelash product. 'You literally paint on false lashes and it costs just $48,' she says. 'I think make-up is recession-proof. Women will never give up lipstick, lip gloss, foundation and mascara. And when the news is depressing, women want something to make them feel better. It's all about feeling good. So we've expanded during the economic downturn and increased our spend on marketing and PR. And it's worked.'

The crisis has made Barrett more creative in her approach to marketing. 'We need to ensure there are value-driven offers—great promotions for gifts with purchase, for example—that draw in more customers.

'We have a promotion running at the moment where customers at David Jones who spend $48 on our products will get a full-size mascara, valued at $28, for free. That is always going to be appealing.'

Barrett says she has looked closely at her costs and cuts back wherever possible to build a buffer against any unforeseen downturn in demand. 'I have looked at freight, travel and administrative costs, but we haven't made any changes to our employee head count or our marketing. It's all about negotiating for smaller quantities and better deals across all of those areas. But given that we're expanding, I'm spending most of my time managing the growth.'

A nice problem to have.

As the mother of two girls aged two and three, Barrett knows the power of the quick fix. Her company has managed to both meet demand and respond to trends faster than other beauty brands thanks to smaller size and greater agility and a determined focus on innovation. 'The business grew organically from the Lash Wands, and a lot of money goes back into research and development,' she says. 'Competing against the rest of the world is part of the challenge that I relish. It pays to be ambitious and actively seize opportunities. I don't feel threatened by foreign competition, and I'm proud that ModelCo is taken seriously in the international area.'

Barrett won the American Express Award for Australia's fastest-growing small business in 2004, and was named Telstra's New South Wales Businesswoman of the Year. ModelCo's foundation was named 'Foundation of the Year' over products by Dior and MAC, 'which was a huge coup for us. I set myself huge goals and find the best team to achieve them.' That still includes her husband and her mum.

ModelCo recently opened a small office in New York; the company is projecting a $12–$15 million turnover and Barrett is planning to make further inroads into the US market with a presence on the Home Shopping Network, where sales can reach $500,000 in one hour. Her airbrush tan range is already available at

Victoria's Secret's in-store beauty bars—where it landed with minimal effort on her part: 'Victoria's Secret contacted us after hearing about our products from a buyer who saw them mentioned in magazines. We'd been tagged as the brand to watch and had won a Newcomer of the Year award. We're fortunate in that we've never had to knock on doors.'

Barrett travels every six weeks to London, Paris and New York, where she occasionally gets an opportunity to buy for herself instead of the company. 'I love bags and shoes,' she says. 'And I love little holidays away. We took the girls to Hayman Island for a five-day break, which is enough for me to rejuvenate. I also have massages in day spas at hotels. As the head of a beauty company I do have an image to portray, so I have to look groomed.'

KERRIE DAVIES

GOLDEN RULES

1. Know your industry.
2. Find great staff and utilise their best skills.
3. Have a business plan incorporating retail plans, distribution and new products.
4. Start small and build.
5. Always find a way—because there always *is* a way.

Chasing Big Bickies

Andrew Benefield
Mrs Fields;
established 1988;
265 employees;
$9.8 million turnover

Photo: Dean Marzolla

Oblivious to the destiny that lay before him, Andrew Benefield was passionately selling the Mrs Fields cookie brand to the public long before he owned it.

As a budding marketing director of a busy Sydney hotel in 1988, he quickly appreciated the power of a tasty treat to woo a client. On his routine visits to travel agents, the newly arrived

Kiwi frequently brought a batch of Mrs Fields' muffins from a tiny store in Wynyard Station as a ploy to win them over. Twenty years later he is still flogging the brand—only in a more official capacity: Benefield purchased the master franchise of Mrs Fields in October 2006.

Unlike his previous retail experience—ranging from the management of 700 Caltex retail operations to owning several franchises—this challenge, he knew, would make or break him. Mrs Fields' cookies were a household name in the US, but the brand's anonymity in Australia was sobering. The company was founded in California in 1977 after a friend encouraged keen cookie chef Debbie Fields to share her gift with the world. She received no such support from her husband, who reportedly told her: 'You're crazy—it will never work.' But after a rough-and-tumble ride through the retail world, Mrs Fields finally sold the business to a US private equity firm in the early 1990s for a cool $330 million. She divorced the husband who failed to believe in her.

It's a story that Benefield is keen to replicate—with one significant difference: not only does the entrepreneur have the full backing of his spouse, also named Debbie, but he is partly riding on her own retail success. 'When we got married, my wife said buying a wedding gown was a stupid way to invest $1500. So she started selling them out of our living room,' Benefield told Sydney's *Sunday Telegraph*. 'From that we built two bridal stores with a turnover of $500,000. She did most of it while I did all the back-room work. We had also accumulated houses and assets, and I had saved a lot from previous salaries. I guess the reality [of being a millionaire] really hit home when we had to cash it all up to buy Mrs Fields.'

'I guess I've always understood that you can't really make serious money unless you go out on your own. At the end of the day, money is just an idea backed by confidence.'

But it had to be done, Benefield says: 'I guess I've always understood that you can't really make serious money unless you go out on your own. At the end of the day, money is just an idea backed by confidence.' Confidence and self-assurance are qualities he has always had in spades, and he has never been averse to taking a risk.

Benefield moved to Sydney from New Zealand in 1988 on a whim, hoping simply to get work. For a while, the prospects looked decidedly poor. 'I almost got down to my last twenty cents and was very nearly on the phone to Mum and Dad saying "Bring me home", before I got a job in a hotel chain,' he says. It was a start—one that opened up a world of possibilities and opportunities for the twenty-two-year-old. Benefield moved up and on to other hotel companies, spent five years at KFC, and headed the retail arm of Caltex's service-station chain. But it wasn't enough. 'Eventually I really wanted to do something for myself that would use my skills. Plus I had done pretty well financially up to this stage, so I started looking for a business that would suit,' he says. 'I really had three boxes to tick. One, it had to be a good brand—and Mrs Fields always has been; I just felt it was undermarketed and underpromoted. Two, it had to have an abundant supply of products. And three, it had to have a positive cash flow.' He paid $2.2 million for the brand and began gearing up to expand nationwide, drawing on his expertise in franchising and letting the possibilities inspire him.

Despite his self-assurance, Benefield knows the road ahead will be arduous as he takes a virtually unknown brand and attempts to etch it into the Australian psyche. So far he has seventeen stores, including three in Sydney, and he wants to make that fifty by the end of 2011. With a tight marketing budget, he will need to be a smart chess player: 'We will have to be tactical and do a lot of sampling and consumer awareness testing,' he says.

The economic downturn has not hit his business too badly. 'We offer a treat, and at $5 people can afford to reward themselves with a coffee and a cookie, even when times are tough,' he says. 'We're not a discretionary purchase in the same sense as a BMW.'

In fact, all things considered the recession has been kind to Mrs Fields: 'Our business grew in 2008/09 by 11 per cent in terms of turnover,' Benefield says. 'We get our ingredients from the US, so we are hit by currency movements, but one of the things we are looking at now is producing ingredients here. They have now agreed we can source our stock in Australia, which will be a great help.'

Benefield is opening another seven franchises in 2009, helped by the growing number of workers keen to control their own destiny. 'There's no such thing as long-term job security any more, so people want to start their own businesses. We had three times as many applicants in 2008 as we had in 2007.'

Benefield says he is exploring new partnerships, including the possibility of inviting different brands into the Mrs Fields premises to help share costs and increase consumer choice: 'It's about maximising returns from the real estate. We can't be complacent, even though we're doing well.'

Benefield isn't quite your run-of-the-mill self-made millionaire. He loves fast cars, but perhaps not to the degree that one would expect. This entrepreneur would rather have an empty garage and focus his luxury expenditure on motor sport. 'What I do for fun is navigate rally cars. I've had the pleasure of navigating for some pretty impressive people—including a past Australian Formula 2 champion and a host of state champions.

'Navigating is very similar to being a franchiser,' Benefield says. 'It requires communicating effectively, telling the driver where to go and how to get there. Then they turn around and blame you when something goes wrong!' As well as indulging Benefield's appetite for risk, his rally-car hobby embodies several of his business principles: 'Enjoy yourself along the way,' he says. 'Believe in yourself.'

Those are messages he loves to preach, especially to his children, who seem to have inherited both their father's zest for life and his interest in what he terms the ancient art of financial success. 'Save,' Benefield instructs. 'I don't consider myself to be a great saver, but I managed to squirrel enough away to enable me to do this. These days, whenever my kids get pocket money, half of it goes into their savings. It is a habit that a lot of us have lost.'

ANDREW CARSWELL

GOLDEN RULES

1. Save, save, save.
2. Enjoy the ride. Enjoy yourself along the way, and don't be too conservative.
3. Believe in yourself and your research. Don't listen to other people trying to give you short-cuts and get-rich schemes. Stick with what you know.
4. Champion those around you. I find that if I make the franchisees happy, that filters down through their businesses.
5. Have confidence. At the end of the day, money is just an idea backed by confidence.

The Unbreakable Bond

Photo: Lyndon Mechielsen

Peter Bond

Linc Energy;

established 1996 and listed 2006; 110 employees; market capitalisation: $1.68 billion

Peter Bond made his first million dollars selling muck. It was dirty, discarded muck, unwanted because at the time nobody thought you could sell it. But Bond had other ideas.

In 1985, the truck driver's son from Camden, in western Sydney, returned from a couple of weeks' holiday to find that his partner had shut down their freight business and sold all the gear. Fifteen thousand dollars in debt and with no job, Bond needed an idea fast. He knew his ex-partner had the contract to remove coal spilled during unloading operations at the Balmain coal loader. He also knew where the coal was dumped. And he had exactly what was needed to turn this dumped filth into a buck: a sharp mind, the capacity for hard yakka, and a rake.

Bond, better known today as the founder and majority owner of $1.65 billion alternative-energy prospect Linc Energy, had found his opportunity. 'In those days they used to clean up coal from the coal loaders and take it away,' Bond recalls. 'They considered it contaminated and wouldn't load it back onto the ship. My former partner was taking it from the Balmain coal loader and dumping it at a quarry at Kemps Creek.' So Bond asked the quarry manager if he could take the coal. Unsurprisingly, the manager said yes.

Suddenly the broke kid had a product. Now he just needed a market. 'I knew hospitals used coal, and I knew brick plants used it,' he says, so he got on the phone. 'I'm talking to this guy trying to convince him to buy it, and he obviously knew I didn't know what I was talking about. He basically told me to f*** off and learn the business before I rang him back.' Bond had a head start, having worked for a couple of years as a trainee metallurgist at BHP's Port Kembla steelworks. He raked up the muck himself and found he had 1000 tonnes. 'I figured about 17 bucks a tonne would see me clear.' Finally, he found a buyer. 'When I got the cheque, I thought, This is the business I want to be in.'

Today that business is like no other.

Bond wants to use the gas locked in the vast underground coal seams in Queensland to make super-clean diesel and aviation fuels. Linc Energy is worth more than $1 billion and his personal stake, a fraction over 50 per cent, makes him one of the most successful of the new energy and resources entrepreneurs. When this book went to press, Bond's demonstration plant at Chinchilla was on the verge of being activated and, if he can get diesel flowing cheaply, efficiently and consistently, then Bond might just become Australia's richest man.

Turning underground coal gas into liquid fuels is a long way from raking up spilled coal. But every good story requires that the hero overcome adversity before he earns his reward. The week Bond was paid for that 1000 tonnes he raked together, the Maritime Services Board put up the Balmain coal-loading contract for tender. Bond bid for it and won, beating all rivals—including the erstwhile colleague who'd left him unemployed. It was a start, but it wasn't long before the young man got his next lesson in business.

Some of his clients couldn't help noticing that their coal-hauler looked as if he lived in his truck. 'They said, "We love your cheap coal, but can you go and get your own house?"' he recalls. 'I was borrowing their front-end loader and borrowing a cup of milk . . . it was second-hand, shoestring stuff. They said, "Can you go and get your own coal yard and actually have a business?"' Once again, Bond's talent for seeing value in the discarded came to the fore.

That first yard was an abandoned site next to the coal rail depot at Glenleigh, near Camden. The site belonged to the now defunct Clutha coal company. So Bond spoke to someone at Clutha and got the go-ahead to move in. 'Unbeknown to me, it wasn't actually their land or their coal, but they'd been asked to get rid of the coal because it was a fire hazard,' he says. So Bond made the coal dump his own. 'That's where I used to park the truck and screen the coal, and that's where I made my empire.' Like the quarry at Kemps Creek, this corner of wasteland was covered with a deep layer of the kind of dross

Peter Bond could turn into a quid. 'They had actually dumped quite a few thousand tonnes of coal there, and it was quite good quality,' Bond says. 'I started with a rake in 1985, and by 1989 I was a millionaire.'

But there was no posturing. In fact, Bond let the milestone pass in silence: 'I paid the house off and the car, and there was money in the bank, but I didn't even tell my wife.'

Bond decided washing coal was the next step in expanding his business and that the way to do it was with a mobile coal washery, which he says was the first of its kind in Australia. Maybe that's why it almost sent him broke again. 'I'd basically bet the million bucks I'd made on it and we were just breaking even,' Bond says. The problem with breaking even was that he had debt—and it was the early 1990s. The credit crisis arrived, complete with double-digit interest rates. It was a period and an experience that permanently coloured Bond's view of Australian banks. 'Out of that, I have no loyalty to any bank,' he says. 'The only exception, and it's going to sound strange, was General Electric. I was in debt to GE Money [the company's banking arm], and they were the

> 'I started with a rake in 1985, and by 1989 I was a millionaire.'

only ones who stood by me. Each time they refinanced me they did it without kicking me with another $50,000 or whatever. So the biggest and supposedly most brutal bank in the world was in fact the best.'

With the help of the Americans Bond clung on, trying to wring a profit from his coal washeries. Then came the really big break: a telegram from an old mate at BHP. 'He'd seen an article about my mobile plants,' Bond says. 'They signed me up to a contract to wash the coal at Appin colliery, behind Wollongong.' A year later, Bond and his new business partner were making a couple of million dollars a year in profit.

They bought a couple of coal mines, including one for about $3 million that they later sold for many times that sum. But by 2002, Bond had had enough. He sold everything and went and sat on a beach in Fiji. He was seeking enlightenment. For a time he wore a Buddhist monk's saffron robe, but he drew the line at shaving his head. He listened to self-actualisation gurus like Anthony Robbins. He listened to Donald Trump, too. Back at home, he got the odd phone call. People wanted him to turn assets around.

Eventually, someone brought him the Linc story. He discussed it with his wife and she told him to go for it.

If all goes well, you can forget about this story. There'll be a better one about Peter Bond—the one about how he made his first billion.

PETER GOSNELL

GOLDEN RULES

1. Know your outcome and what success looks like before you start.
2. Know the basic steps to achieve that success and look at each step as a mini business plan.
3. Surround yourself with extraordinary people.
4. Back yourself and have total belief that you can achieve success.
5. Be passionate about what you do.
6. Know your exit strategy before you start.
7. Be generous. Leave money on the table and give back to the community.

A Winning Flight Of Fancy

Hans Hulsbosch

Hulsbosch;

established 1986;

twenty employees;

$10 million turnover

Photo: Frank Violi

Half a century ago, in a quaint village in the dormant south of the Netherlands, a young Hans Hulsbosch was sketching his first picture. Despite living a world away from Australia and having never set foot outside his low-lying country, the boy drew a little kangaroo.

Fast forward to the present, and Hans is still drawing kangaroos. But bigger—much, much bigger. On the tails of Qantas jets.

When Hulsbosch was asked to redesign the famous flying kangaroo logo for Qantas, he couldn't help but reminisce about his debut drawing. The revamped Qantas logo and the recently relaunched Woolworths logo are the latest in a long line of successful ideas from the creative minds at Hulsbosch, the design company Hans launched in 1986.

Redesigning Qantas's kangaroo, one of the world's best-known logos, was not the first time he had dealt with the airline. In fact, it was Qantas that helped launch Hans into the cut-throat Sydney ad industry.

Hell-bent on living in Australia since childhood, he'd initially migrated with his wife to New Zealand.

Despite being a designer of some note—he'd created the packaging for Willem II, then the world's largest cigar manufacturer—Hulsbosch was repeatedly turned away from the Australian embassy in the Netherlands.

'When I said I was a designer, I think they laughed. When they needed carpenters and plumbers, I guess designers were last on the list,' he recalls. The newlyweds had to become New

Zealanders before they finally got approval to live in Australia, but Hulsbosch says it was 'worth the sacrifice'. By then they had two children. Arriving in Sydney, they wasted no time setting up their new life. Within two days, the Hulsboschs had an apartment in Mosman filled with new furniture from David Jones, and Hans had a prize job at the prestigious ad firm Clemenger. 'As soon as I arrived, I just started knocking on doors,' he says.

At Clemenger, 'I had the best time. Those four-and-a-half years there were just phenomenal. Probably one of my favourite ads was for Tia Maria. That campaign was one of the first in the world for a product apart from tourism that became a global one. I was travelling a fair bit, and you'd be going through Rome or New York and there would be your ad on a billboard. It was a great feeling.'

But despite the praise, the salary and the lifestyle, something was missing—design. Hulsbosch was mad about design, but the giant ad firm didn't see it as overwhelmingly important. So he did something he was already quite accustomed to: he took a risk.

'I went to the management and said, "We are doing something wrong. What we are missing is a design arm in the agency." They were already doing design in Europe on a small scale, but all I heard back was, "Mate, there's no money in it. Go and do some ads."

'So I thought, here is an opportunity, I'm going to do it. And I made the decision to move out and start my own business.'

A tiny office in North Sydney was to become Hulsbosch's first home. The four-metre-square box contained a desk and chair, a fax machine, a photocopier and a phone. But within a year Hulsbosch had five or six staff, a new office and, more importantly, two of the biggest clients he could have hoped for: Qantas and giant cruise operator P&O.

'I couldn't have had a more fantastic start. Once Qantas and P&O walked in the door, I'd made my first million within about a year and a half.'

'I couldn't have had a more fantastic start,' he says. 'Once Qantas and P&O walked in the door, I'd made my first million within about a year and a half.'

Today, his latest Qantas and Woolworths logos hang proudly in Hulsbosch's plush Mosman office, alongside designs for clients such as Taronga Zoo, Nylex, Foxtel and Oatley Wines.

Hulsbosch says keeping designs and thinking fresh is the key to surviving when the economy takes a dive. Businesses, he adds, must stay relevant so they are poised to lead the way when the recovery starts. When that happens, 'It is going to be tough, because there will be fewer companies and they'll all be fighting for business. So you need to make sure you are sending out the right signals.' To keep work coming in, Hulsbosch has been cutting its rates. 'We have had to become a lot more flexible—some of our clients are not doing so well, so it is about helping them get out of the current situation.'

Rebranding, he notes, is not just about logos. It is about the company's whole image. Hulsbosch cites McDonald's as an example. 'They are keeping the store designs fresh, and now you can buy a meal for a dollar. They really get what is happening in the economy and are responding to it.'

Hulsbosch says Woolworths' 'fresh, inviting' green logo is already paying dividends, and store design has also helped. 'You always want to invite people in through the fresh produce section and make sure it is presented in an attractive way. It sets the tone for the experience and gives the whole shop a "fresh" feel,' he says.

These days at Hulsbosch, cash flow is king. Hans is keeping a closer eye than ever on incomings and outgoings, but he is still expanding and still hiring: 'The economic downturn is a great time to look for new staff, because when the economy is booming, you just can't find anybody.'

He says his clients are wonderfully loyal. Take, for example, his most recent encounter with Qantas.

'I was called over to [chief executive] Geoff Dixon's office. He stands there and says, "As of today, you've got the business. Have a look at the identity, see if it still applies. If you think it needs to change, go and sort it out. But don't come back with the wrong thing."'

Judging by his record, Hulsbosch couldn't do the wrong thing if he tried.

ANDREW CARSWELL

GOLDEN RULES

1. Nothing happens without a brilliant, committed team.
2. The goalposts change every day, and you must be able to change rapidly.
3. Never underestimate the value of loyalty.
4. Never let the competition know what you are doing.
5. Always be thinking about how you can make your brand better than the competition.

The Day That Changed A Life

Margot Cairnes

Zaffyre International;

established 1986;

thirty employees;

$10 million-plus turnover

Photo: Anthony Reginato

Sitting outside a kiosk on one of Sydney's northern beaches, Margot Cairnes had no inkling that her life was about to change forever. It was 1985, and she was up to her neck in debt, unemployed, bringing up two children alone and nursing her dying father.

Desperately in need of a break, she'd decided to have a 'rich day' with her kids. 'We were really,

really, really poor,' says Cairnes. 'But we test-drove a Jaguar, then went to Double Bay and tried on beautiful clothes we couldn't afford. Then we went to the kiosk at Manly's Shelly Beach and I had a glass of champagne and the kids had a glass of pink lemonade. I said to the kids, "One day we'll be rich."

'My ten-year-old daughter looked at me and said, "Mummy, we already are rich. We have each other." I was speechless. I felt about two inches tall.' At that moment, Cairnes resolved to work hard when she could and be happy with what she had. Not long after, her father passed away. It was time to find a job.

Years before—while still in her early twenties—the trained teacher had moved from Sydney to Darwin and landed the top position in a child-care company. Taking charge of five child-care centres and three family day-care schemes with more than 1000 children, Cairnes jumped into the deep end and survived.

'I had also trained as a psychotherapist,' Cairnes says. Now a mother and deep in debt, 'I had to decide what to do with all my qualifications. But I couldn't decide—so I made it up. I started my own company and just went out to do something that hadn't been done before.'

Cairnes created her own brief: a consultancy

that would improve managers' self-belief and relationships with their staff and in doing so help companies reach goals they'd previously seen as impossible. She says it was 'pure luck' that two men from Victoria's Portland aluminium smelter heard her giving a speech. 'They liked what I said, introduced me to their boss, and that led me to where I am today,' she says.

Cairnes took seventeen managers from the smelter on a camping trip through central Australia, on small boats down the then-flooded Cooper's Creek. 'We were gone for ten days, and I called it a leadership training course,' she laughs, admitting that she made it up as the group went along. 'The first night out we camped on mud flats without tents. Me and seventeen men, most of whom snored,' she says. 'In the end, it changed their lives—and the way they ran the smelter.'

Cairnes said it felt as if she'd 'found the cure to organisation cancer'. After that, things happened fast. 'I started to get headhunted.' She worked for the Reserve Bank of Australia and for BP, both in Australia and in Europe, helping with a merger with Mobil.

Cairnes' debts had been more than paid off by this stage, and her first million was racked up before she headed overseas. She allowed herself a moment to reflect back on that day at the beach.

'I was sitting at my home in Clontarf on the balcony, looking at the water, holding a first-class ticket to go to London to stay in the Ritz Hotel. I thought, "This is it, I've done it."'

Cairnes also bought herself a BMW and—as she still does today—indulged in natural therapies as a reward for all her hard work. 'I love massages and going to spas, and I'll often go to health retreats just to spoil myself,' she says.

I was sitting at my home in Clontarf on the balcony, looking at the water, holding a first-class ticket to go to London to stay in the Ritz Hotel. I thought, "This is it, I've done it."

At first she resisted hiring staff and setting up an office, but the business was expanding so fast she couldn't avoid it. She finally set up Zaffyre International in the late 1990s. Fletcher Challenge Energy chief executive Greig Gailey had worked with Cairnes on the BP–Mobil merger. Now in New Zealand, he asked her to come and work with him. 'He said: "I need to turn around a whole company, so I need you to have a company",' recalls Cairnes. 'That was when I started to recruit other consultants.

'I just didn't have it in my blood to build the company before that point. [Growth] wasn't my driving force. I just loved doing what I did and it made me a lot of money. I get my thrills working as a consultant. As soon as you have a whole lot of other people working for you, then you are really doing something else.'

She soon found herself jet-setting on an almost permanent basis. 'One year I was out of the country for thirty weeks. I was working with Levi Strauss in the US, BP in London, and Fletcher Challenge in New Zealand.'

An unspoken partnership started up and, each time Gailey moved on to restructure a new company, he took Cairnes with him. Other major corporate clients include Zinifex, Origin Energy, Western Power, Alcoa and Telstra. With twenty-five staff and an office in North Sydney, Zaffyre continues to do consulting work throughout Europe, the US and Australia and is currently experiencing a resources boom of its own in Perth. 'On a good day I walk into the office and there are about three people here because the rest are consulting all around the world,' Cairnes says. 'These days I myself mostly work with just a handful of managing directors and boards.'

So is retirement on the cards? Not likely, she says: 'I tried to retire and it didn't work. At the time I'd become tired of going to work. I suppose I got run down and burnt out and I tried to disappear to Byron Bay. In the end I had a year off, but that gave me a chance to change my attitude. I had a year of doing yoga, going to the gym, going to the beach and finding a new husband.'

Cairnes now has a house in Annandale, Sydney, and a holiday house at Byron Bay, where she spends a week every month writing books. She has six under her belt already, including *Boardrooms that Work—A Guide to Board Dynamics*; *Staying Sane in a Changing World* and *Peaceful Chaos*. As to the failed retirement, Cairnes has no regrets. 'The company went on, of course, but not as well as it would have if I'd been here. Now that I'm back, it's just sky-rocketing, and I'm having a ball.'

And there's a new challenge down the track. 'When you see people come to life and reach goals they once wouldn't have dared imagine, it is really exciting. I'm very keen to take what we do to more companies. But I also want to take it into communities. There's no reason why a government couldn't do this and take the whole country to a new level. If you can get an entire community to go through this process, the social good is just colossal. That is my dream.'

Given her track record, there's every reason to believe she'll make that dream, too, come true.

RHYS HAYNES

GOLDEN RULES

1. It all starts with you, but relationships are key.
2. You cannot change anyone else, but change yourself and you will change all your relationships.
3. Challenge, change or accident: treat everything as an opportunity.
4. Dare to dream—the same old expectations lead to the same old outcomes.
5. Be grateful for everything that happens to you. That's the way you learn what is real success.

An Idea Awash With Cash

Photo: Ella Pellegrini

Jim Cornish

Ecowash;

established 2004;
six employees,
125 franchisees;
$8 million turnover

Jim Cornish's first word was—if only his parents had known—a partial prophecy.

'It's absolutely true—my first word was "car",' Cornish explains. As it turned out, he was just one word—'wash'—short of predicting his fortune. It wasn't all that long before little Jim was driving cars. 'My mum used to race cars—she was the New South Wales hill climb champion back in the 1960s. I started nagging her to teach me to drive when I was very, very young. She taught me when I was about four or five,' Cornish recalls. 'I had my schoolbag behind my back so I could reach the pedals.'

Cornish, thirty-eight, didn't become a Formula 1 champion, but he did get into car racing in a big way, competing as an amateur in the Super Touring category at Bathurst in 1997, '98 and '99. His career followed a very different track: 'I did three years of veterinary science and then an extra research year in combination with Taronga Zoo, on the reproductive physiology of exotic species,' Cornish says. 'So, basically, giraffe shagging.'

But the Dr Doolittle experience, which took up six years of study, was always a sideline to Cornish's driving ambition: running his own business. 'It was something I always wanted to do. I set up my first business when I was eighteen, six months into my first year at uni,' he says. 'I set up one of those video game entertainment centres, back when they were cool. I had to get a $15,000 loan, for which my parents went guarantor, but I made the money back very quickly.'

After just a year, the owner of a chain of pinball parlours offered to buy him out. 'He came in and told me I was running it all wrong, and maybe he was right,' Cornish says. 'I hate inefficiency and wasting money, so back then I thought, Who comes to a pinball parlour? Kids from school! And because we wanted to be socially responsible we didn't open until 3 p.m., so kids couldn't wag school to come in. Anyway, this guy changed all the rules, and he went bust within a year.' What Cornish learned from the experience was how to run a business by thinking like a consumer. That wasn't hard, because he enjoyed playing his own machines after closing time.

Cornish finished his vet science studies, then went straight back to school to do an MBA. 'I've always had this thing about time. Mates of mine took two years off and went to Europe, but I never did any of that. I just wanted to get it done and get on with it,' he says. Still racing, and by now a sponsored driver, he was also working full-time in the pet-food industry, for Nestlé. Then, in 2004, his life changed overnight.

Cornish's car, 'a black Monaro that I valued more than anything in my life . . . er, except my loved ones, of course', was serviced by a mate named Stewart Nicholls. 'He called me up and said he wanted to wash my car, but he wasn't going to use any water. I said, "No way, don't you dare touch it."

'But eventually he talked me into letting him show me how this product he'd found worked. I was so impressed we teed up a meeting the following day with the people who were looking at importing it. We told them: We're going to have mobile car washing and franchises—just give us a year of exclusivity. It all happened literally overnight. I rang my accountant that day, we went and saw the lawyers, and we set up a company. It was that quick.'

'It all happened literally overnight. I rang my accountant that day, we went and saw the lawyers, and we set up a company. It was that quick.'

Nicholls shut down his garage immediately, and the pair mortgaged their homes so they could buy a brace of Daihatsus and paint them bright orange. Ecowash—the waterless car wash—was born. The secret of the waterless wash is a polymer product originally imported from Monaco. 'You spray it onto the car and it actually lifts the dirt off the surface and encapsulates it. The polymer acts as a lubricant. There are no petrochemicals in it, so it leaves the car polished and protected because a layer of polymer stays on the car.

'I was going to stay at Nestlé because I had a good deal there but it just got too busy, so six weeks later I resigned,' Cornish says. While a waterless wash has big appeal in drought-prone Australia, the Ecowash brand was actually launched before widespread water restrictions hit. 'The line we used is: "The indulgence of a clean car, with a clean conscience",' Cornish says, 'but we didn't market ourselves as an environmental solution. Any business needs to be sustainable, so it was part of our core business strategy rather than a marketing strategy.

'We also came into the market at quite a premium: you can get your car washed for $12, and we charge $35, so there had to be more value for customers than just feeling good about saving trees. That's where the quality and convenience came in. In some of our overseas markets, like France, there is no water issue, but it's been taken up just as quickly there.'

Now, a premium car wash is one of the first things you'd expect to be cancelled when people start counting their pennies but Ecowash has continued to grow, in terms of both franchisees and customers, despite the credit crunch.

Even Cornish isn't certain why.

'We've had some corporate clients cancel on us, particularly in America, but business is up, and some of our franchisees are booked out for two months in advance.'

Cornish suspects several things are working in his favour: 'People aren't buying cars like they used to, so maybe they're looking after them better. Then again, there are lots of people selling cars to save money, and they want them looking pristine to get the best price. We're getting business either way.'

Another factor may be time: 'I'm hearing about people working longer hours to keep their jobs or earn extra money, so they don't have time to wash cars themselves.'

France is just one of fifteen countries that Ecowash has expanded into, and global growth has remained steady despite the economic downturn.

'Australia's been one of the toughest markets to crack,' Cornish says. 'We're naturally a cynical nation, I think.' The company operates in the Middle East and Central America as well as Europe. In the US, 'We went in expecting there to be competition, but there's nothing even close to us. But because of the recession we are underperforming on our targets there, though we're still growing healthily,' Cornish says.

A big problem in the US and Australia has been not finding more franchisees—the company is deluged with applications—but finding franchisees who can get funding from the banks. 'Banks have become much more cautious, and even though you need only $45,000 or so to start a franchise they are reluctant to lend.'

The cash crisis prompted Cornish to take a close look at the business and strip out unnecessary costs. 'We used to advertise in almost every franchising magazine and on every website, but we analysed where we were getting the best applicants from and focused our money there, cancelling the other advertising.'

Cornish has also found many companies and organisations keen to form partnerships and alliances during the downturn—pooling resources to secure discounts. 'We just formed an alliance with the American Automobile Association, which has millions of members. We've also started an arrangement with Holden National Leasing, and with Leaseplan in Greece. It's a great time to hammer out these sorts of deals.'

> 'You have moments where you sit back and go, Wow, how cool was that?, but we still put everything back into the business. It's not a feeling of arrival, it's a feeling of being well on the way.'

Ecowash cracked its first million in just its second year of business, thanks to a customer base that is 70 per cent female, and turnover is now $7.5 million. But Cornish hasn't seen fit to reward himself for his success—yet. 'I'm notoriously bad at that. I'll set goals like, "When we get to this point, I'll do this." And then we get there I go, "Nah, that was a stupid idea, let's just keep going."

'You have moments where you sit back and go, Wow, how cool was that?, but we still put everything back into the business. It's not a feeling of arrival, it's a feeling of being well on the way.'

Cornish says his job doesn't feel like work any more: 'It's become a lifestyle.' Fortunately, that lifestyle still includes his first driving passion: cars. 'I just love cars—not just fast ones. I've got a four-wheel-drive now and I even love driving that. Anything with wheels and a motor—I'm hooked.'

STEPHEN CORBY

GOLDEN RULES

1. Choose something you can be passionate about.
2. Build systems. Simplify every process and make sure it can be duplicated.
3. Fix things once. Multiply every problem by 100 before starting on the solution.
4. Look at where you are getting results and focus resources there.
5. Be honest and open with your staff. Communication is critical.

A Fascination With Figures

Photo: Angelo Soulas

Angus Geddes
Fat Prophets;
established 2000;
thirty-five employees;
$5 million-plus turnover

There's something strange, almost freakish, about highly successful city businessmen. Very often you find that before they applied their nuclear-powered brains to finance they studied quantum physics, built their own computers or wrote papers about how to solve Rubik's cubes, things that are incomprehensible to most people.

By the time he turned twelve, Angus Geddes had memorised the names of every director of every company on the New Zealand stock exchange. Rain Man would have been proud. 'I was just fascinated by investing,' he recalls. 'I'd read every company report to soak up all the information I could. I read annual reports from cover to cover.' That same year, Geddes decided that the savings he'd put in the bank weren't returning enough interest. So he became an investor. 'In the early 1980s, interest rates in New Zealand were pegged at about 2 per cent, and I'd saved up a couple of hundred dollars. I told my dad, There has to be a way of getting a better return on my money. So we went to the stockbrokers to open an account.' By the age of sixteen, Geddes had turned his $200 into $40,000.

'I'd read every company report to soak up all the information I could. I read annual reports from cover to cover.'

'I made some extraordinary calls,' he says. 'And I had some luck. But I also had a good broker who gave me some good steers that chimed with my own judgment.' That was the era of *Wall Street* the movie, yuppies and the 'greed is good' mentality. But for Geddes, it was never about the money. He claims never to have aspired to big houses or flash cars. He drives an eighteen-year-old Mercedes 560SL which, he says proudly, has appreciated in value.

For Geddes, everything is about value. He won't fly first class because he doesn't think it's worth it, but does fly business because it delivers comfort at a reasonable price. His investment approach is the same. He looks for out-of-favour companies that have been underperforming the market for an extended period and are, in his view, underpriced. Then he invests, waiting for a turnaround in sentiment to take the share price back up. The approach has served him well for two decades, although it took him six years to recover from the 1987 market crash.

In the early 1990s, Geddes travelled to London and New York and worked in stockbroking, gaining valuable experience that he put to good use when he arrived in Sydney in the mid-1990s. 'I took a job at a small brokers on full commission—no salary at all—and I hit the Yellow Pages, cold-calling professionals like doctors, lawyers and accountants. I asked if they'd be receptive to good investment opportunities, and I would often leave them with a tip. They'd see the company do well, and that would get them interested. Many of those clients are still with me.'

At the time, Geddes says, he was a bit of a

maverick: 'No one was doing that kind of cold-calling in Sydney—but I'd seen the guys on Wall Street doing the same thing. It's hard, but it worked. Within six months, I was writing $300,000 to $400,000 of business a year, taking home the best part of $200,000.'

Soon afterwards Geddes was headhunted by BT Financial, where he stayed for a couple of years before moving on to broker JBWere. His value-investing approach meant standing firmly against the trend. 'Back in 2000, when the technology bubble was inflating, everybody was piling into it. But I just knew it was going to crash. You see, I'd seen it all before, in 1987, when I lost a huge chunk of my own money that I'd spent half my life accumulating. That really hurt. And I could see all the warning signs again: hugely overvalued companies based on virtually no earnings, massive speculation, the madness of crowds. It had gone crazy.'

While many of his peers were cheerleading for high-tech, 'I was advocating gold and energy stocks, both of which had been completely out of favour and were coming out of long bear markets. I think a lot of people thought I was a bit mad. It turned out to be a great call, because gold and value stocks such as energy companies did exceptionally well.'

Geddes tried to get his clients out of tech and into these value stocks, but was largely ignored. 'I showed them graphs of the '87 crash and the past and present Nasdaq index, and said the same thing was going to happen, but most of them were so sold on the tech story they'd just go and buy tech stocks through another broker,' he says.

That was a turning point for Geddes, who found the experience so exasperating that he decided to quit. 'I just thought that I'd be better off backing my own ideas: starting my own newsletter and website where I can write my thoughts down and clients can read it or throw it away, but I'm not going to go hoarse on the phone every day giving people advice they're just going to ignore. It's tough as a stockbroker, because you're interacting with people's greed and fear, which are very intense emotions. It can be exhausting, like banging your head against a brick wall, especially if you're a contrarian investor like me.'

' It's tough as a stockbroker, because you're interacting with people's greed and fear, which are very intense emotions. '

Geddes set up his own independent research house and named it Fat Prophets. Thanks to some astute stock-picking, his small base of initial subscribers quickly expanded—to the surprise of some early nay-sayers: 'People thought it was crazy to call ourselves Fat Prophets, because it's a bit "out there" and not very conservative; they said investors wouldn't trust us. And they were probably right in the very early days, but we soon made some good calls and our reputation started growing.'

Although he had been earning good money for some time, Geddes says it wasn't until 2002–03, when the business had gained some momentum, that he made his first million—a combination of his personal share portfolio and the value of the business. But his response was just business as usual: 'I certainly didn't stop and think that I'd made it, or that it was any kind of milestone.'

The business was so successful that Fat Prophets opened an office in London and now has a funds-management arm as well as a listed investment company with $50 million under management. Geddes has also launched a popular range of so-called separately managed accounts: preselected portfolios of shares for investors. And soon he wants to launch a hedge fund.

His mantra, 'There is no such thing as failure in business,' has made him fearless, giving him the drive to make Fat Prophets a truly global brand and the belief that he can. So what is Geddes investing in now? Not property, that's for sure. 'I sold my apartment in 2003 and have used the money to much better effect by investing in equities,' he says. 'You're better off renting and investing your money in shares than buying a property right now. Why buy an underperforming asset that might yield 2 per cent when you could get into shares that will give returns of five or ten times that much? I think residential property prices are at risk: interest rates are going to rise, and in eighteen months or so I think you could see prices falling and some good buying opportunities springing up. But I won't be buying anything till I see some value in the market.'

When Geddes says his investing philosophy is not about the money, that isn't entirely true. It is about the money, but as an abstract score rather than hard cash. The dollars he earns are just points in a big game called Success in the City. All Geddes wants is to be right, see his theories borne out and prove his critics wrong. So far, so good.

NICK GARDNER

GOLDEN RULES

1. Follow your passion. If you're passionate about making a sandwich, open a sandwich shop.

2. Be prepared to work like hell.
3. Surround yourself with excellent people—people as smart, if not smarter, than you who complement your skills.
4. Don't be afraid of failure—there is no such thing as failure in business. If you go down a path and it doesn't work, go down another path; you will always find a way. Once you lose the fear of failure you can do anything.
5. Maintain your focus and the determination to achieve what you want.
6. Have fun.

A Career Well Matched

Photo: Frank Violi

Trudy Gilbert
Elite Introductions International;
established 2005;
five employees;
$1.2 million turnover

Money can't buy you love, or so the saying goes. But whoever dreamt up that one hadn't met Trudy Gilbert, Sydney's Cupid and boss of the most successful upmarket dating agency in town.

For $2695 she'll make sure you have at least six dates in six months, though it's unlikely any-body will need that many: nearly 90 per cent of her first introductions choose to see each other again. For her, love is half the reward: 'It's been amazing. It's just so satisfying when you get a call to say they're moving in together or are in a serious relationship. I feel like I'm making the biggest difference to people's lives.'

Clients can put the six-month membership on hold for a maximum of two years if they start seeing somebody regularly. It's a concession Gilbert regards as practical as well as ethical. 'It wouldn't be fair to meet somebody on a first date, see them for six months, then have your membership expire. My business has grown by word of mouth so I want my clients to be delighted with my service.'

And selling love seems to be recession-proof. Despite the global downturn, Gilbert's business has soared. 'I think the crash caused people to re-evaluate and become less materialistic,' she says. In the good times, 'A lot of people made and lost a lot of money, but it didn't make them happy. So I think they started asking themselves how they could be content. And for many the answer was with a fulfilling relationship.'

Gilbert, who had her first child, Siena, in June 2009, and now has an office in Melbourne and is eyeing Brisbane as the next location for her growing empire.

'It's actually a great time to be an employer because I've got such a wide choice of potential employees,' she says. 'Office space is cheap, it's cheap to advertise if I need to—all in all, it's a really good period for the business. It shows there are growth opportunities even in recessions. You mustn't be afraid to expand just because the economy as a whole is stalling.'

Gilbert is a natural matchmaker. She got the idea for Elite Introductions after arranging twelve of her friends into six happy couples. Two couples are now married, and one guy has bought an engagement ring and is plucking up the courage to propose. 'I'm good at seeing what makes people tick. After putting so many of my professional friends together, I thought I could make a go of this as a business. I started researching the market and realised that nobody was really catering for people like them—or me. I read about a company in America that was introducing members of New York high society, which obviously works because you're introducing like to like. So I applied the same principle to professionals and executives in Sydney.'

If this hadn't been a winning formula, Gilbert would have come up with something else. She's one of those idea-a-minute types, fizzing with barely contained enthusiasm and infectious self-assurance, something she deems essential to any budding entrepreneur. 'You have to be confident and present a positive image to staff and clients. You are the embodiment of what you want your company to be, and your staff will draw inspiration from that.'

Gilbert grew up in Sydney's eastern suburbs, the daughter of a clothing sales agent. Naturally charismatic and witty, her father would take her out to work with him. The experience showed her that work could and should be fun. 'It was just like he was going out and visiting his friends. Every visit to every retailer was full of laughs and good humour. It didn't seem like work at all.' Her mother stayed at home while Trudy grew up, but then became chief executive of the synagogue near their home in Rose Bay.

'I get the business side from my mum and the people skills from my dad,' Gilbert says. 'After seeing how he worked, I knew I wanted to run my own business. And when I left university and took a job in marketing for a hotel group, I found the bureaucracy frustrating and the work politics a waste of time and resources.' She soon got fed up and, aged just twenty-three, went to Italy. After a stint back in Sydney and some more unsatisfying jobs she returned to Italy, where she was hired as a communications consultant, teaching companies how to improve their sales and marketing techniques. 'After a while I thought, Hang on! I could do this on my own. I don't need to be working for this company.' So, at twenty-seven, she started out on her own.

'It was a great success. I had clients including Ferrari, Dolce & Gabbana and La Perla. In my three years in Italy, I managed to save $50,000.'

> 'I get the business side from my mum and the people skills from my dad.'

Then she returned to Sydney to settle down. Two months after arriving in Sydney she met her husband, Philip. 'We were set up by a couple that I'd set up together. Three months later, Philip and I were engaged.'

The marriage has lasted, and matchmaking is also going well. Elite has more than 500 clients, split pretty evenly between men and women. But even those who stump up the full membership fee are not guaranteed admission to Gilbert's books. She turns down up to 30 per cent of applicants. 'I am judged by the quality and integrity of my clients,' she explains. 'I deal exclusively with highly intelligent, successful professionals. If somebody doesn't fit the bill, for whatever reason, I won't take them on.'

She doesn't have to give out much dating

advice, because her clients are savvy and successful with good people skills. But still, people make mistakes. 'Very often men talk about work too much or hog the conversation. I tell them: Be positive, don't talk about the mad, the bad or the sad in your life. Put your best foot forward and give the best possible impression.' Another tip she says works wonders is for the man to pay the bill without the woman's knowing: 'It's a really smooth move to just slip the waiter your credit card on the way to the bathroom and have the bill settled so that when you go to leave, it's completely seamless. It makes you stand out as a class act.'

As for her first million, Gilbert made that in 2005 just after she turned thirty-four. 'I knew we were close to it, but my accountant rang to congratulate me,' she says. 'I promised myself that I'd be a self-made millionaire by the time I was thirty-five, and I've done it with time to spare. My husband and I are going to the W hotel in Bali to celebrate.'

Gilbert doesn't attribute her happiness to money. 'Success is not about money. You need to be happy about who you are and what you have. My parents instilled a fantastic work ethic in me and I am so grateful, because thanks to that it doesn't matter if I have money or not. They've made me a confident and rounded person who's comfortable in my own skin, and that is what really counts.'

NICK GARDNER

GOLDEN RULES

1. Do something you truly love—your excitement and energy motivate people around you.
2. Have a clear vision and create a solid company culture where employees feel valued, heard and rewarded.
3. Be self-confident but humble, and commit yourself to a life of constant learning and development.
4. Treat people with dignity and respect, and maintain uncompromising integrity in everything you do. Giving honest value earns you respect.
5. Be recession proof. Don't be at the mercy of fashion or fickle trends.

Success On The Line

John Ilhan

Crazy John's;

established 1991;
800 employees;
$200 million turnover

Photo: Alex Coppel

Think about how much of your working life is spent sending and reading e-mails, then try to guess how many hours a day a platinum-level chief executive like 'Crazy' John Ilhan is tied to his keyboard.

Try none. And that's not because the mobile mogul has chosen to retire and consume some of his $300 million-plus fortune. No, the Melbourne-based Ilhan simply refuses to use a PC, hasn't had one in his office for more than five years, and blows a raspberry at the idea of a BlackBerry. 'Honestly, I wouldn't even know how to turn a computer on any more. If I pretend to use one at work the guys all start laughing because they know I've got no idea,' he explains.

Ilhan booted out his computer because 'I was losing so much of my day on it, losing business partners, losing staff,' he says. 'I like to communicate by vision, by sight and verbally, and I thought, I can't keep doing this. So my executive assistant, Amanda, took over. She reads everything. She knows what I'm thinking and how I do things.'

E-mails are presented to him in point form, and Ilhan says everyone gets a response of some kind—he just doesn't have to write it. He's not big on paperwork, either. 'I'll never read anything longer than three pages. I'm not good with detail,' Ilhan admits. Avoiding both forms of mental clutter frees him up for the important stuff: 'It means I get to spend time doing the things that really matter. I'd rather go around and visit stores, meet with staff, get involved in training, be with the guys on the front line, give them motivation.

That's my drug. I was tied to the office. Now I enjoy my job a whole lot more.'

> It means I get to spend time doing the things that really matter. I'd rather go around and visit stores, meet with staff, get involved in training, be with the guys on the front line, give them motivation. That's my drug.

For Ilhan, it's always been about the personal touch. He has the patter of a lifelong salesman but little of the impersonal fakery most people associate with that role. In short, he's convincing. He must have been compellingly so back in 1991 when, aged twenty-five, he set up his first mobile-phone shop. It contained precisely zero mobile phones—except his own. 'I only had $1000 in my pocket. I borrowed about $2000 off Mum and Dad to buy a phone, and a lot of my mates were tradesmen so they helped build the place, which was basically just a bench with brochures,' he says. 'I had enough money in my pocket to buy one phone at a time—they were thousands of dollars each still at that stage. So I just sold off brochures. I'd sell a phone, shut the shop and drive to the city and buy it for the customer. I had to sell myself, because that's all I had. I was a bit naïve and young and stupid because, when you worked the numbers, how could it work? But when you believe in yourself it's not the numbers that matter, it's about, "I can sell. People like me." It's that young, naïve attitude, and you just work like crazy.'

Ilhan, the Turkish-born, fiercely proud Australian whose real first name is Mustapha, hasn't eased up on the work ethic since. Initially, he laughs off suggestions that he once worked eighteen-hour days. 'No, it wouldn't be that much. Let's see: I start at 7 a.m. and it would only be, um, sixteen hours a day. But then I do usually go until midnight, so it probably is eighteen hours. Oh my God! That's a lot . . .'

But it's mostly recreation, he explains: 'When you do something you love, it's not really work. And I've been doing it for sixteen years—it's just part of what you do. I've been lucky, I've chosen a field I love, so it's not work. I love dealing with people. I love the challenges of growing a business. It's like a work of art—you always try to improve it.'

After dropping out of university two months into an arts degree, Ilhan took a temporary job on the Ford production line in his home suburb of Broadmeadows, Melbourne. He ended up staying more than three years but left after becoming frustrated that graduates were getting promoted and he wasn't. A job came up selling phones at Strathfield Car Radio, and as soon as Ilhan started he knew he had found his calling. He quickly became the company's top salesman. Then a dispute over his commission payments made him so angry he walked out—and set up his own shop, right across the road.

After building a loyal base of customers, he got his big break when Telstra offered to back his business. By 1994 he had half a dozen stores in Melbourne, a rate of growth he now realises was excessive: 'I relied on relationships and handshake deals rather than contracts. I grew too quickly and then Telstra changed its strategy and cut our commissions and I didn't get paid for about six months,' Ilhan recalls.

While he was feeling the pressure financially, his personal life also hit rock bottom when his brother committed suicide. 'At the same time, the competition really hated my guts and they used to leave threatening notes on my windscreen saying, "You're finished now." It was a tough time,' Ilhan says. 'That was 1996, and I'd already made my first million, but then I very nearly went bankrupt. I was in administration, so I lost all that. The first million was the hardest to make and the easiest to lose.'

The experience taught him some hard but valuable lessons. 'After that I realised my own weaknesses and I employed people with finance backgrounds. I ended up being the visionary and employing people who could get me to that vision.'

The only hurdle Ilhan still had to clear was his business name. Telstra execs were not big fans of the Crazy John's label. 'They hounded me, saying it was unprofessional and it wouldn't work. That went on for years, but they were so wrong,' Ilhan laughs.

By 2003 he was on a roll, opening seventy stores in eighteen months and crushing all rivals—including Strathfield Car Radio. Ilhan then found himself at the top of *BRW*'s Young Rich List in 2005, with a fortune estimated at $300 million. 'It was funny seeing that, considering what I had started from,' he says. Success had crept up on him: 'You just work hard and the rewards come. It's not like winning Lotto overnight—you don't think, Wow, I'm rich! I only really noticed it when they mentioned it but, being a bit competitive, I did like being No. 1. The $300 million figure was right at the time. It's a bit more now, but in the end you don't work for the money. At the start you do, because you have to pay the bills. But after that it becomes about challenges and success.'

Ilhan clearly remembers the first thing he

bought when he started feeling rich: a second-hand, smashed up brown Porsche 930. 'When I was sixteen I said to Mum, "One day, I'm going to have my own business, a house by the beach and a Porsche!" I couldn't afford a new one, but I loved that car. I never did buy a new Porsche.' Instead, Ilhan now drives a Bentley, after ditching his Lamborghini. He's also got the $15 million home by the beach, in Brighton, but the house he's proudest of is the one he bought for his parents, with whom he lived until he was thirty. 'I built them a new house in Broadmeadows because they refused to move; they thought it was a big thing just moving across the suburb,' he says.

'It was wonderful to be able to do that for them. I wouldn't be here if it wasn't for their support. They said, "If you fail, there will always be a bed here for you—we're always behind you." And that support was crucial, because I knew if I failed they'd still love me—so I could try anything.'

Stephen Corby

GOLDEN RULES

1. Always have humility.
2. Be compassionate.
3. Be ruthless with your business strategy, but not with individuals.

4. Always give back to the community.
5. Whatever you do, pick something you love and never, ever give up.
6. Take risks and learn from your mistakes.

ADDENDUM

John Ilhan died shortly after this interview was first published, in October 2007.

His 75 per cent stake in Crazy John's automatically passed to his wife, Patricia. She held on to it for a while but, with four children under ten, keeping it on the fast track proved too much.

Ilhan was replaced as chief executive by Brendan Fleiter, who had worked with him since 1996. 'The whole company was in shock for a while,' says Fleiter. 'So many people knew him personally, and his very first employee still works here after seventeen years. So it was a personal loss as well as a professional one. But we knew that if he was watching, he'd want us all to get on with it. He would have thought it was a great branding exercise—great publicity. I joked with staff afterwards that the one day he got his face on the front page of all the papers, he wasn't around to see it. But he would have wanted everybody to keep the business growing.'

A year after Ilhan's death, his wife and other shareholders sold the business to Vodafone

Hutchison. 'The slowdown has hardly hit us at all,' says Fleiter. 'Mobile telcos is a very defensive place to be, and we are still expanding with new products such as pre-pay and contract mobile and broadband services.'

Ilhan, it seems, put Crazy John's on a sound enough base that it can get along calmly without him.

A Life Of Talking Points

Photo: Alan Pryke

Alan Jones
Occupation: broadcaster

If you think interviewing Alan Jones would be slightly intimidating, you're wrong. It's very intimidating.

Normally in interviews—particularly the ones conducted by the king of the airwaves himself—the interrogator is seen as the attacker. Even when he's being interrogated, Jones seems unable to get off the offensive. It quickly becomes clear that he is unsure why the interview has been scheduled. Then, after a glance at my notepad, he says: 'And you've got too many questions there. I won't be answering all of those, but away you go.'

A question seeking his opinion of ABC-TV's *Media Watch* elicits the response: 'I don't think about it. I don't watch it. Like most Australians.' As to whether Jones, like fellow talk radio star John Laws, sees himself as being outside any code of ethics because he's a broadcaster rather than a journalist: 'I'm not a journalist. Nooo. Never.' But there is some safe ground, such as the remarkable career that, from a late start in radio at forty-four, brought him to his present apogee of wealth and influence.

Born in 1941 and raised on a dairy farm in rural Queensland, Jones remembers 'drought and poverty. It was terrible,' he says. 'Heat and dry, and cattle dropping dead.' His mother was a teacher for the deaf and blind, and he would eventually teach too. 'She had very high ideals about teaching as a vocation, and I suppose she persuaded me. But coming from where we were, I wasn't exposed to many vocational choices,' he says. Jones was sent to boarding school at thirteen, but says that doesn't mean his family was wealthy. 'I went to a private school because there were no other schools, and my parents gave up everything so I could do that, and died never having had a holiday in their lives.'

The transition from boarding-school student to teacher was smooth, and in 1970 Jones was poached from Brisbane Grammar by the King's School in Sydney, where he became an extremely successful rugby coach. Five years later Jones was asked to leave the school under something of a cloud but, typically, he doesn't see it that way. 'I don't think I ever intended to be a teacher all my life. I soon saw that there was a bit of a ceiling there—you could only go so far. At King's I had in fact taught the son of the Deputy Prime Minister, Doug Anthony, and that's how my movement into politics occurred,' he explains. 'Three times I've been a candidate for parliament, and they were sensible enough to reject me.'

He may not have been elected but he was noticed, and in 1979 he was hired by Prime Minister Malcolm Fraser as a speech writer. 'Fraser was a very loyal Australian. Obviously we would have had our differences, but I don't ever talk publicly about them,' Jones says. The work was 'night and day, with no sleep', but was it making him a millionaire? 'A what? Oh, come off it,' he snaps. 'What makes you think I'm a millionaire now?' (An attempt to interject something about his rumoured $5 million-a-year salary is met with a disbelieving snort before he powers on.) 'I was on $42,000 a year. And Malcolm Fraser was always borrowing money. He never had any on him, and he'd always be asking me for $50, and I didn't have any money to my name. I remember once he paid me back—$12.80 it was, and I kept that cheque. One day it'll be an auction item.'

From 1981 to 1985 Jones remained a non-millionaire, working as executive director of the Employers' Federation of New South Wales. His side job, as coach of the Wallabies national rugby team, paid nothing at all. Jones is voluble on what makes him a great leader of men: 'I think I can say, modestly, that my teams mostly won. If I've got any ability it is that I can get the best out of people. And I can get people to go beyond what they think they're capable of.'

In 1985, out of the blue, 'without ever having been in a radio station', Jones was offered a job at 2UE. 'Program director John Brennan said, "I think you should be on radio"—and it all took off at a cracking pace,' he says. A deal was struck on the back of a serviette at a Chinese restaurant, and while Jones won't say what numbers were written on the napkin, he was soon after more. 'David Maxwell [the then general manager of 2UE] started talking about ratings, and

I said nothing because I had no idea what they were,' he says. 'So I raced out to John Brennan and asked what these ratings were all about. I said that I can't even have an intelligent conversation unless I know what's this ratings stuff.'

By the next meeting, Jones was ready. When he was told that his ratings were 'terrible, only twos or threes', he asked what would be considered good. 'Maxwell said: "If you got ten, I'd die and go to heaven." And I said, what incentive is there to get ten? And he said: "Listen, if you get ten by the end of the year, I'll give you a $100,000 bonus." I'd never seen $100,000 in my life. I'd never seen anything with six figures in it. And we got to 10.2 in the second-last survey, and they came and gave me this cheque. It was quite something.'

The next payment that blew Jones's mind was so big he felt compelled to record it. 'It was when I came to 2GB from 2UE [in 2002]. The deal was that I'd get some of the money up front, and I photocopied the cheque.' So, were there six zeroes on it? 'Oh, my God, no. There were six digits, but not six zeroes. Oh, no!' he says. 'I also photocopied the cheque I got for the Golden Slipper [won by his horse, Miss Finland] because I couldn't believe the Sydney Turf Club was writing a cheque to me for that amount of money. I think it was $3 million.' Though Jones professes surprise that he's perceived as a millionaire, it seems safe to deduce that he passed that mark somewhere between the start of his radio career and 2002.

Jones also struggles to remember the first extravagant thing he ever bought: 'I have no idea,' he says. 'No. I think I most probably sent my father to the Melbourne Cup. He always wanted to go. I always thought if I had money I would send him and gave him the real royal treatment.' He himself has pretty modest tastes, he says: 'I've never been one for extravagance. I don't need the best phone or to be at opening nights in black tie. I hate black tie. I get criticised because I spend all my money on other people. I think I give a bit too much away. But I say to people, none of these things is worth two bob unless you share them. The only thing that gives you any pleasure is sharing. I've got a lovely place down in the Southern Highlands, but the greatest satisfaction I get is when others are sitting in front of the

'I've never been one for extravagance. I don't need the best phone or to be at opening nights in black tie. I hate black tie. I get criticised because I spend all my money on other people. I think I give a bit too much away.'

fire having a drink and I know they could never afford to be there [on their own account], but they're loving it.'

Jones believes there are three things that make a man feel rich: 'If you can drink whisky out of a crystal glass, you've got an air-conditioned room, and you've got a housekeeper to help you with all that drudgery, you're a millionaire,' he says. 'So that makes me a millionaire.'

What he makes strenuously clear is that he's earned everything he has. A self-confessed workaholic, he gets up at 2.30 a.m. every day and never, ever gets even five hours' sleep a night. 'Whatever money I've got, I've rolled up my sleeves. I've got up at two o'clock and I've put the light on before anyone else, and I turn it off after anyone else,' he says. 'There are no shortcuts in this sort of stuff. All this talk of luck is nonsense. You've got to make your own luck.'

> 'If you can drink whisky out of a crystal glass, you've got an air-conditioned room, and you've got a housekeeper to help you with all that drudgery, you're a millionaire. So that makes me a millionaire.'

So, after what could be described as a colourful career in radio, does he have any regrets? 'Look, I don't live in the past,' he fumes. 'We all, in life, have ups and downs, and who am I to live in regret? There are people out there who can't walk, who can't see, who can't hear, who can't talk, who've never been to a restaurant, who've never got a passport. Who are we to be living in regret? We're very fortunate. Very privileged.'

STEPHEN CORBY

GOLDEN RULES

1. Don't expect others to do what you should do for yourself.
2. The only thing you get without hard work is failure.
3. Enjoy things—successful people are those who enjoy themselves.
4. Be decisive. People fail because they're wishy-washy. Stand for something.
5. Share. If all of the above produces anything, share it.

A Cut And Dried Success

Denis McFadden
Just Cuts;
established 1990;
1500 employees;
$80 million-plus turnover

In 2007 Denis McFadden thought he was in trouble. The bank had called. His presence was required in the city. It sounded bad. But this was *the* Denis McFadden, founder of the Just Cuts hairdressing franchise. Whatever the problem, he would answer the bank's summons with shoulders squared, chin up and hair gelled.

Something was a little odd, though. The

meeting would not be in the bank manager's office. Instead, he was to present himself just after midday at Times on the Park, an upmarket steakhouse in Sydney's Sheraton Hotel. When McFadden arrived, he found two other bank clients already there. 'I realised I was sitting around the table with some very wealthy individuals—and it dawned on me that I must now be classified in the same way,' he says. Far from being in trouble, Denis McFadden had arrived. He had attained the level of affluence at which bank managers cast off their polite indifference and adopt a solicitude bordering on the obsequious.

Two months after he was born, McFadden's father died. About the next ten years he says very little. His formative years, as far as he's concerned, didn't begin until he was eleven, when his mother married a Qantas pilot. 'I benefited from a wonderful life from then on,' he says. Most of his youth was spent in the United Kingdom and he began working in London as a hairdresser, later opening his own salon in Marble Arch, at the top of Oxford Street. 'It was the Swinging Sixties, and we were doing Lady So-and-so and also doing the nannies, so it was a real mix of people,' he says. Clipping the locks of English aristocrats kept McFadden in London for ten years.

During that time he married an Englishwoman who already had two daughters. They had two sons together, and in the late 1970s the family came to Australia after deciding it was a better place for the children to grow up. McFadden began cutting hair at Hurstville. 'In those days, there was either a basic barber shop or the full-works chemical salon—nothing in between,' he says. 'So, I started in 1983 with the idea of something in the middle—something with broader appeal.'

His idea came to him when Hurstville Council ran a promotion to get people to shop locally. McFadden painted a sign on his window that read: 'If you're paying more than $6 for a haircut, you're getting clipped.' More than 100 people trooped through the door that week. 'I'd seen these people before. They had come in and asked if we did dry haircuts. I'd say: "No, I'm an artist. I need to wash it and I need to blow-dry it, and it's going to cost you." But these were busy people, time poor, and all they wanted was a haircut. I realised after that promotion that there was an angle here, a need in the community for people who just wanted a haircut.'

He later moved his main business to the new shopping centre at Hurstville. With him went the sophisticated equipment and the clients who made appointments. But, with three months remaining on the lease at the old premises, he put up a sign saying: 'Just Cuts—$7.' While he indulged his artistry at his salon, he didn't abandon his cost-effective cutters down the road. He devised little scripts for them to deliver so they could glean information from the people responding to the $7 enticement. McFadden wanted to know about these customers. Who were the people who didn't care that much about their hair? And why were there so many of them?

At this point in the late 1980s he still saw his full-service salon as his core business. But McFadden would soon down tools forever. He looked at franchising and went as far as meeting people who were in the business, but he wanted a simpler business model. His first franchisee was a young hairdresser who worked for him. After she approached him with the idea of starting out on her own using his Just Cuts model, her father, a wealthy property developer, asked McFadden about franchising agreements and business manuals. McFadden got busy writing and came up with a simple formula. 'What we came up with was a fixed fee—equivalent to just twelve haircuts a week,' he says. 'That first franchisee had to give me cash for twelve haircuts a week, and I think at the time a haircut was $11.'

So in 1990 he became a franchisor. 'I wanted an easy life, but I knew the only way to do that was to have lots and lots of franchisees. The way I've done that is by working out what my franchisees wanted.' In the early days, they were interested in lifestyle. 'I had single mums with four kids, and all they wanted to do was spend time with their kids,' he says. 'Today it's slightly different. They've got expenses. A big house and a mortgage. Kids in private schools. They say they need to earn $150,000, $200,000 a year and that's difficult in franchising. We can't guarantee something—they could come back in a few years' time and sue us. It's making it more difficult.'

So, with the economic downturn McFadden decided to make some changes: 'While everybody was hunkering down, we got Saatchi & Saatchi on board for a rebranding exercise. Like Woolworths, we wanted a new image to ensure we're looking fresh when the recovery kicks in.'

The business he's in may be a perennial, but he can't afford to be complacent. 'The good thing is that hair grows in good times and bad, but it's become more competitive. We are in a number of shopping centres, and shoppers have dropped off, so our business has suffered a little in some locations. We've had to move a little up-market and compete not so much on price but on service. It's crucial that we stay fresh and relevant for the next ten years.' Meanwhile, the company was still about 10 per cent up in the 2008/09 financial year.

McFadden is closing two salons, which he says were not performing very well anyway, but he'll be opening three others in different locations, all with the new logo and store design. He is also expanding his product range—offering DIY salon-standard colouring kits for just $14.95, instead of the $200 charged for many in-store colouring services.

'It's about being convenient, competitive and innovative,' he says.

As for new franchisees, he continues to receive between two and four applications a week. They pay between $150,000 and $200,000 up front to invest in Just Cuts. The company has a small consortium of banks prepared to lend 50 per cent to franchisees, and the owner has to find the balance. The money pays for the shop fit, a month's rent in advance, furniture, the grand opening strategy and McFadden's fee. The average Just Cuts franchisee owns 2.4 outlets, although one owns fourteen, and 70 per cent of franchisees own more than one outlet. 'It's not about ego, it's about making money,' McFadden says.

And making money he is, with 174 salons in Australia, New Zealand and India. Multiply the 150 salons in Australia by the $288 a week they pay him and McFadden's local owners are bringing head office more than $43,000 a week. Throw in the twenty-three Just Cuts franchisees in New Zealand and the newly opened New Delhi Just Cuts, and the artiste from Marble Arch looks to have shorn franchising's golden fleece very deftly indeed. 'I needed the numbers to make the money, and when there are 174 of them it adds up.' Keeping costs down is not too hard, either. McFadden has seven people in his office. There are no auditors policing his franchisees, and he keeps in touch with them through meetings of the franchisee advisory council, which meets about five times a year.

'I needed the numbers to make the money, and when there are 174 of them it adds up.'

The most visible sign of his personal success is the thirty-two-hectare property he bought two years ago in the New South Wales Southern Highlands. While he might be a hairdresser, McFadden likes his fun. He's got a chainsaw and tractor, quad bikes and motor bikes, and he works three days a week, from Tuesday to Thursday. If his banker wants to take him to lunch in the city it will need to be on one of those days.

PETER GOSNELL

GOLDEN RULES

1. Use an economic downturn to refresh your branding.
2. Always consider change—don't get stuck in a rut.
3. Do your homework.
4. Think about your business in a global sense.
5. Be passionate and think big.
6. Give your clients what they want, and they'll give you what you want.

A Fine Performance

Andrew McManus
Andrew McManus Presents;
established 2000;
eighteen employees;
$80 million turnover

It turns out that all the stories are true. Sometime Mötley Crüe drummer Tommy Lee really is the hardest-partying man alive. Rock promoter Andrew McManus has the bruises to prove it. 'Tommy and I hit it off last time they were here and we got lost for three days and nights,' McManus groans. 'He just wanted to keep going.

He was too good for me. I had to put the white flag up—I just could not continue. Normally I hold my own with these guys, but he's a character and a half, that one.'

Drinking with—and trying to rein in—the baddest boys of rock is all part of the job for McManus, but he says the hardest partiers he's ever handled are not rock stars but wrestlers. Back in 2000 he and the manager of Kiss, Doc McGee, saw an opportunity to take wrestling to Europe. They scooped up fifty-eight 'big, kooky guys, including a guy called Big Poppa Pump, some midgets and some female wrestlers' from World Championship Wrestling. 'They party really hard—how they do it has got me,' McManus laughs. 'And then they have to go to the gym and train during the day. After the wrestling, they're just on this huge high and they go and hit the clubs. Boy, do they hit the clubs.'

McManus and McGee basically bought WCW and enjoyed twelve months filling arenas in Europe before the ka-ching king of wrestling, Vince McMahon, realised they were eating into his potential and started sending his A team over. 'We were like a twenty-pound monkey fighting a 500-pound gorilla. He just ate us up,' McManus says. It was one of the few times in his high-voltage career that McManus has been forced to take a backward step.

Surprisingly, McManus is not a frustrated rocker. 'My uncle had a pub, and from the age of twelve or thirteen I just wanted to be a hotelier. I really liked the lifestyle and his ability to come and go and make money.' At seventeen, he enrolled in a four-year trainee management course and so impressed his teachers that he was fast-tracked, graduating after two years to become an assistant manager in Townsville. At twenty-one he was given the Rose Bay Hotel to run, making him the youngest licensee in the country. 'It was mine for eighteen months and I was loving it. We took it from doing twenty-seven grand a week to sixty-something grand. But I outsmarted myself. We were making so much money the owners sold it out from under me, and I was out of a job.'

Fortunately, one of McManus's bookmaker contacts heard of his predicament and set him up with a job at the Coogee Bay Hotel. 'They rang me up and said, "Do you know anything about music?" And I said, "Absolutely nothing," and they said, "Neither does the guy who's running Selina's. When do you want to start?"' That was 1981. Over the next seven years McManus grew the live-rock venue into a Sydney landmark—and a huge money-earner for the hotel.

In 1985, one of his regular bands, The Divinyls, asked for help because they weren't seeing enough profit for their hard work. 'They told me they were doing all this work but never making any money,' he recalls. 'I said, "Give me three shows and I'll show you how to make money. You get $20,000, and I'll keep anything we make over that." They didn't believe we could even make twenty, but we made $47,000.' He went on to manage the Divinyls for seven years—during which time they had an international hit with *I Touch Myself*.

By 1995, McManus was ready to move on. He took a year off, his first real holiday ever. 'I just wanted to chill out and I could afford to do that, but I certainly wasn't a millionaire yet—nowhere near it. The Divinyls thing was just part of the training,' he says.

During his long break, he considered his options. 'I had no degrees or schooling. The only thing I had was my little black book, so I rang some friends and asked them what to do next.' Someone suggested becoming a promoter. Crooner Barry Manilow happened to be in need of one, so McManus established the International Touring Company. ITC became such a success it was bought out by Abigroup, which then sacked its founder in 2000. 'I remember thinking, It's my company, how can they do that? And forty-eight hours later I'd set up Andrew McManus Presents.'

The next year, McManus came up with the idea for Kiss Symphony. That was his breakthrough, he says: 'the highlight of my career, and when I made my first million'. Fortunately, he was already mates with Kiss. 'Gene [Simmons] and Paul [Stanley] are great businessmen. They jumped at the idea of putting the Melbourne Symphony Orchestra in Kiss make-up and going orchestral. We made the first million that night and I was very proud to get 37,000 people along to one of my shows,' McManus says.

The promoter, who nominates a white Rolls-Royce as the first extravagant thing he bought, believes most modern rockers take the Pearl Jam approach and run their bands as businesses. Some never grow up. All they want is drink and drugs. With bands like that, 'you can't give them too many days off because they'll go and get on the soup, so you might lose them'.

McManus has also seen his share of weird riders over the years (the list of demands an act sends out in preparation for a tour). 'Stevie Wonder just loves to take the p***. He always asks for purple and orange towels, for example. Stevie Nicks wanted a certain running machine on a certain floor of Crown Casino so she could look out the window while she was running and see the view.' Of course, he was more than willing to accommodate the whims of her band Fleetwood Mac, who provided his company with its biggest ever earn: $14 million from fourteen sold-out shows. McManus's other proud record is for the biggest take from Sydney's Acer Arena in one night: $3 million, thanks to Luciano Pavarotti.

> 'Stevie Wonder just loves to take the p***. He always asks for purple and orange towels, for example.'

The financial crisis has knocked the business around, slashing older audiences in particular. 'They've been hit hard with their income and their super funds, so they're not spending,' he says. 'Youth acts are still going strong because the audience is young and living at home so they still have spare cash.'

McManus has cut back on costs as much as possible and is taking a far more conservative approach to his business than he is used to. 'I should probably have battened down the hatches more quickly, but I booked New Kids on the Block and they failed dismally, even though my research suggested they should do well. We took a big hit there,' he says.

'Now I am being more careful, and more sensitive about the price we charge for tickets. You can put people off even the biggest names by charging too much.'

McManus says he is now expanding the business, focusing heavily on 'viral' marketing campaigns, which are cheap but enormously effective when they work well.

The promoting game is not all hanging out with famous people and scraping the cream off their profits. 'It's a very risky business, and there are too many promoters at the top level. If you won't pay enough for a particular band, someone else will,' he says. 'It's all about the money—no loyalties in this business—and you can find yourself paying too much and losing money. And yes, tragically, that's happened to me.

Bands like Kiss and Fleetwood Mac are different, he says: 'They have a loyalty, and I know what they're going to need financially. I'm not going to say I'm blessed, but I've had a very good run, and made some very good friendships, and it's from them that the opportunities come.'

Besides cars—he has a Bentley and a brace of Benzes to go with the Rolls—McManus's other extravagance is gambling. Just last weekend, he won $154,000 on the Geelong/Melbourne Storm double. He is, it seems, a man who just can't lose—unless he goes drinking with Tommy Lee.

STEPHEN CORBY

GOLDEN RULES

1. You are what you think. No matter what, have no regrets.
2. Never look back, only forward.
3. Money alone will not make you happy. The biggest thing, outside of the comforts that money can bring, is friends. Surround yourself with good people and you will be a wealthy person.
4. Be innovative with your marketing.
5. Life is full of choices, and you are the only one who can take responsibility for those choices.
6. Be flexible and ready to change along with the economic climate.

The Boss With The Lot

Photo: Dean Marzolla

David Michaels

Bite Me Burger Co.;

established 2007;
eighty employees;
$18.5 million projected turnover for Bite Me and two other enterprises

From Las Vegas casino king to Sydney burger baron, the roles come like courses for entertainer turned entrepreneur David Michaels, founder of Sydney's newest fast-food outlet, Bite Me. Life seems like one long banquet for the British-born businessman, who models himself on Richard Branson and enjoys at least two lunches and two dinners a day. 'Sometimes I'll have six meals—then a cocktail party after that,' he admits cheerfully. 'Eating out is my pleasure.'

He's gained a couple of kilograms since opening the first Bite Me burger bar in 2007, but Michaels's smallish frame is only slightly rounded. His shape and his relentless energy convey only rude good health. Maybe his hectic lifestyle helps keep him trim. Bite Me—at Star City Casino—sprang from his early assessment that Sydney suffered from a lack of good burgers—a view many may hotly dispute, especially outside the inner city.

His open-plan, first-floor office in Paddington hums with activity. At one table three women, dressed in carefully casual chic, discuss arrangements for a cocktail bar. Topics include the relative merits of wooden cocktail crushing sticks or muddlers as opposed to stainless steel ones. At another table staff from Michaels's design company, BEE (Brand Environment Experiential), are busy preparing material for various projects, including Michaels's ice-cream brand, Pat & Stick's. In the lane downstairs, a fleet of Smart cars in red and black Bite Me livery stand in a neat line.

Michaels, who shares Branson's fascination with the power of brands, is primarily a design guru, but he began his business career selling breathalysers. 'I made my first bit of money when I was nineteen in England,' he says. After ditching theatre school the brash lad from north London approached a financially troubled manufacturer, offering to shift its surplus breathalyser stock in return for a 50 per cent share. The company agreed, and Michaels says he made his first million pounds repackaging the devices and selling them as Christmas-stocking fillers. Within two years the money was gone—blown on boats, cars, friends, jewellery and houses.

> 'I'm no good with money. I'm a creative person, an ideas person. I'm not a financial person.'

'I don't regret that,' he says. 'It was part of being young. But blowing a fortune helped to teach me about my own limitations. I'm no good with money. I'm a creative person, an ideas person. I'm not a financial person. So ever since then I've surrounded myself with good people who can take care of the parts of the business that I'm not so good at handling. The finances and cash flow are among them.'

He left for the US in his early twenties, landing first in New York, then in Los Angeles, where he ended up as a staffer (or 'cast member') at Disney. Despite his complete inability to draw and lack of any formal training he quickly became involved with the company's design team, producing concepts for new theme parks and other projects.

Later, in Las Vegas, a combination of design nous and fast-talking bravado gave him entrée as a design consultant to the city's lucrative casino industry. 'Las Vegas is an amazing place,' he says. 'I ended up spending a lot of time there. I just wanted to learn what makes the whole Vegas model tick.'

Something of the theme-park casino—with an inner-city twist—has found its way into Bite Me. The menu, developed with prominent chef and food writer Kim Terakes, includes the Beef Encounter, Soft Prawn and Pluck Me (chicken). A concession to the local burger culture is available in the Great Australian Bite—'one with the lot' to you and me. It turns out to have all the right ingredients in a slightly narrower and substantially taller package—about 12 cm high, with a Bite Me flag stuck on top. Chips arrive crammed into miniature shopping trollies. Michaels admits to a certain bemusement at the Aussie burger: he doesn't like beetroot and doesn't understand the inclusion of pineapple.

He doesn't quite understand how he became so rich, either. 'I can't attribute the success to any one thing,' he says. 'It's really been a combination of a whole load of projects and businesses and fingers in different pies.' Despite being worth many millions of dollars, Michaels says he doesn't regard himself as wealthy: 'Wealthy to me means Bill Gates and Donald Trump. To me, it's not about the money. It's about the game—the fun of building something new. Money gives you freedom, and that's great, but I want to get up every day and create something. That's what makes me happy.'

For Michaels, who works 'sitting cross-legged on the floor and drawing in my head'—leaving trained designers to finish the job—concept is the key to success. 'If I had to say what I am more than anything else, I'm an ideas person,' he says. Friends—and the chance to buy an apartment on Kent Street with views of King Street Wharf on one side and the Opera House on the other—brought him to Sydney, but he remains a man of international horizons.

'Wealthy to me means Bill Gates and Donald Trump. To me, it's not about the money. It's about the game—the fun of building something new.'

Rejecting the franchise model, he plans more wholly owned outlets in Australia before taking the brand to China, the US and Europe. More casino projects in Macau and Las Vegas also keep him constantly on the move, as do plans for a return to the theatre with a massive ice production, billed as *Cirque du Soleil* meets Torvill and Dean.

Although he enjoys a party and clearly knows how to have a good time, he doesn't seem the type to lapse into extended bouts of relaxation. Among Michaels's few private passions is television: *EastEnders*, *The Sopranos*, *Boston Legal* and *Oprah* are particular favourites.

He seems to mean it when he insists it isn't all about money, that if business isn't 'fun' it isn't worth doing. 'I don't know whether it's being a driven person, or being stark raving mad,' he laughs. 'Nothing's ever done. It's always a work in progress, and I'm learning every day.'

JIM DICKINS

GOLDEN RULES

1. Relationships: It's crucial to get on with the people you work with and go into business with. If the chemistry isn't there, forget it.
2. Passion: I have to be able to be passionate about my work, so it has to interest me. If you said we could make a fortune selling air conditioners, I wouldn't be interested. It's too dull, and life's too short.

3. Innovation: I need to create new things, to be imaginative and not have that constrained. Always dream to the fullest, then pull back if you have to.
4. Fun: If it isn't fun, then there's no point to it. I want to get up every day and enjoy it.
5. Diversity: I know it's a cliché, but variety is the spice of life. I love to have a variety of projects on the go and different challenges to meet.

X Marks The Spot For A New Approach

Jennifer Nielsen
X Inc. Mortgage Brokers Loan Market Group
established 1995;
600 employees;
$42 million turnover

Photo: Warren Clarke

When twenty-three-year-old home-loan queen Jennifer Nielsen went to the bank in 1982 for her first mortgage, she co-applied for the money with a single female friend who also wanted to secure an asset before a husband. 'I don't know if the bank manager thought we were lesbians, but I recall he thought it very odd,' Nielsen recalls with amusement. 'Now, it is very common for friends to buy property together.'

The unconventional loan application was accepted, and the block of land she and her friend bought was Nielsen's first step towards making $1 million from shrewd property trades in the lucrative Brisbane and Sydney markets. 'I love to buy and sell real estate and I've done well out of it, especially in Queensland. But Kenny Rogers, in the song *The Gambler*, had it right—you never count your money when you're sitting at the table.'

Having experienced the satisfaction—and financial benefits—of putting her money into bricks and mortar, the chief executive of X Inc Mortgage Brokers is helping others to do the same in a complex lending environment now overshadowed by credit-crunch anxiety. Despite the uncertainty, X Inc—which effectively doubled its market presence by merging with Ray White Mortgages last year—is employing up to thirty new brokers a month. Nielsen and her business partners John Kolenda and Dean Rushton aim to make theirs the biggest mortgage broker in Australia by 2010. 'We want to have a mortgage broker attached to every real estate office in the country,' she says.

So how did she make the leap from young

home-buyer to mortgage magnate? 'It's tempting to believe that success is due to individual brilliance or a magic formula,' Nielsen says. 'In reality, it comes down to hard work and, in our case, identifying a gap in the market. We wanted the white-collar market—the AB demographic. We made a difference for them. Now, it's far more acceptable for those people to go to a broker for a loan.'

'It's tempting to believe that success is due to individual brilliance or a magic formula. In reality, it comes down to hard work and, in our case, identifying a gap in the market.'

And in tough times such a service is all the more welcome. 'People need to talk to someone like a broker to understand the finance options and what is likely to happen, because it's confusing. They are turning to mortgage brokers for objective advice.'

She sounds as if she's been in finance all her life. But Nielsen's first jobs could hardly have been further away from that world. She worked as a cook and deckhand on a tiger-prawn trawler in the waters between Cairns and Groote Eylandt. Then she was a regional sales manager for Yellow Pages. Both jobs, however, taught her how to run a business and inspire other people. 'On the trawler, I learned about teamwork. I can't claim it was as bad as the *Deadliest Catch* TV show or anything, but there were situations where, if someone didn't do their thing, the boat could literally sink. At Yellow Pages I was a benevolent dictator, but I learned to listen. I had no choice.'

Nielsen went on to become a recruitment consultant and worked closely with Kolenda and Rushton, executives at the time with Aussie Home Loans. In 2004, they asked her to join them in setting up X Inc. She trusted their knowledge enough to concentrate on learning. 'Their competence took enormous pressure off me,' Nielsen acknowledges. 'It's much harder learning a new industry at the top than from the bottom. It changes your leadership style because the people around you know more than you.'

Nielsen applies the lesson she learned on the prawn trawler to the fast-paced world of finance. There's a captain, but when you are riding the waves it's all hands on deck. 'We have built our brand on limited funds,' she says. 'We were taken to court [by Aussie Home Loans for poaching staff] when we were less than two minutes old, and a major bank wouldn't work with us until that case was resolved.' Now it seems to be plain sailing, but the same principle of equality continues: 'I have an open-plan office. I personally return calls. I think having a personal assistant is a luxury rather than a necessity. And when you surround yourself with assistants, they are between you and the real world.' Nielsen shares a PA with three other managers.

Having a child has also changed Nielsen's management style. Commuting between Brisbane and Sydney, she travels with her four-year-old son and a nanny, who cares for him in the flat above her Surry Hills office in Sydney. The experience has made her deeply sympathetic towards employees who also have young children. 'I scheduled my Caesarean, then I couldn't control it [child rearing] any more! When a staff member has a child-care issue, I now say, "Bring them into the office." If that had happened before, I'd have been mentally counting the lost productivity through gritted teeth. Now I know. The biggest challenge has been to balance my business life with my young son and my husband—who runs a global business of his own. I love my family, and I honestly believe balance is important.'

KERRIE DAVIES

GOLDEN RULES

1. Stay close to the people who are close to your customers.
2. Treat every customer as if he or she is the last one you will ever get.

3. Keep all your key intellectual property in-house. Don't outsource it.
4. Be aware of, and stay on top of, what your competitors are doing.
5. Believe above all else that there is a solution to everything.

ADDENDUM

In October of 2007, X-Inc merged with real estate chain Ray White Group's Electronic Mortgage Organisation Channels of Australasia Pty Ltd (eMOCA), comprising Ray White Financial Services, Loan Market and REA Home Loans, to create a $13 billion loan book.

Nielsen headed the new entity, commonly known as the Loan Market Group, but stepped down in January of 2009 to focus on developing Ray White's online marketing strategy. She is currently head of online marketing for the Ray White Group.

Success All Wrapped Up

Michael Paul
Pack & Send;
established 1993;
240 employees;
$35 million-plus turnover

Photo: Dean Marzolla

A successful entrepreneur needs many qualities: passion, patience, determination, a willingness to make sacrifices and belief in your idea. Michael Paul has all of them in spades.

Had he listened to conventional wisdom when hawking his idea in the early 1990s, Paul would have thrown in the towel. Fifteen years on he's boss of Pack & Send, a multi-million-dollar, award-winning, Australian-based empire that is taking on the world. His idea was simple: to take awkwardly shaped, valuable or delicate items that are a nuisance to mail, pack them professionally, take care of all the paperwork, and ship them anywhere in the world.

The business was already thriving when eBay came along, but its advent has been a godsend for a postage company specialising in bulky, fragile and irregular items. Paul said shipments of goods purchased on eBay account for about a third of Pack & Send's business. But it was several years before he was in a position to capitalise on the online auction-room's emergence.

Paul has spent most of his working life among parcels. His career began in a post room at the pharmaceuticals company Richardson-Merrell (now Marion Merrell Dow), where he learned all the ins and outs of postage and packing—and a little about logistics. After rising to a management and logistics role he took his expertise to a series of other firms, continuing to learn as he went.

Paul was working as a freelance logistics consultant in the early 1990s when he had his eureka moment. The problem: how to send a desktop computer from Sydney to Melbourne.

It doesn't sound like rocket science, but at the time Paul thought it was close. 'I couldn't find appropriate packing materials, or a carrier that would pick it up,' he says. 'I had to do all the paperwork and find a way of getting it packaged properly. It turned out to be a two-day exercise. It was crazy. Why wasn't there a place I could go and just drop it off and let them do all the work? It seemed such a blatant gap in the market.'

To discover what might plug the hole, Paul travelled to the US. 'They did have companies that packed and posted items for you, but not as well as I planned on doing it, so I was absolutely determined to come back to Australia and make a go of it.' He set about looking for freight partners—and immediately hit resistance. 'There was a lot of scepticism. One senior executive took me aside and said: "Michael, Australians will not pay for a convenient packing service." He said he'd been in the industry for thirty years and that there were "limits to what you can do in this market". Well, I didn't agree with that at all. In fact, I thought the opposite. There are no limits to what can be done. That made me more determined than ever.'

Paul was so determined that he sold his house, moved in with his in-laws, and borrowed from family to scrape together enough money to open his first Pack & Send store in Parramatta, in Sydney's west, in 1993. On his first day of business, he made one sale—of a cardboard box, priced at $2.90. 'I've still got the receipt from that day to remind me how far we've come, and never to lose faith,' Paul says.

It wasn't exactly a flying start. He and his wife Susan 'wore out many pairs of shoes' pounding pavements, knocking on company doors explaining their service and putting flyers in letterboxes. It was hard work, but the idea took off. Within a year, the store was turning over $200,000 and expansion beckoned.

'The store was doing really well, but I always had a vision to take this right across the country,' Paul says. 'It was never going to stop at one outlet. We knew we had a fantastic business model with high gross-profit margins. The challenge was to replicate it on a national scale.' That's when they thought about franchising. 'This type of business is all about personal service and going that extra mile. That's our real selling point. It's difficult to get employees to go that extra mile for customers. That's why franchising—effectively giving them their own business—really works. Then they have the incentive to do it.'

His first franchisee approached him in 1994. He was the regional sales manager for Startrak, at Crows Nest in Sydney. The outlet is still there today. There followed a decade of heavy investment in infrastructure, computers and technology, including legal work on contracts and franchisee agreements, a national marketing campaign, and a buying department to source and negotiate prices for supplies for the franchises. The program required a huge amount of funding, which Paul had to borrow.

By 1999, Pack & Send had twenty franchised stores. In that same year, two pivotal events took place. First, Paul was approached by businessman Barry Smorgon, who shared Paul's enthusiasm. He invested enough in the company to cover many of its infrastructure needs. Then eBay launched in Australia, and that changed the face of the business. 'Suddenly, we noticed a big change in consumer behaviour,' Paul says. 'People everywhere had awkwardly shaped objects they needed to send around the world. And there we were, perfectly placed with a national network and well-thought-out infrastructure. It was a godsend.'

Today, a quarter of Pack & Send's franchisees own multiple outlets, and some have made millions in their own right. 'It's wonderful to see,' Paul says. 'One couple worked very hard and borrowed to buy their first outlet. Now they have three, and they own the premises as well.'

And there will be more to come. Paul has set a goal of opening 1000 stores around the world. He has started a master franchising operation in Britain, where his first store is booming. New Zealand has also seen its first successful Pack & Send opening, and Canada, Singapore, India, South Africa and mainland Europe are also targets.

During 2008/09, Pack & Send grew by 40 per cent. If the financial crisis is to blame, then financial crises should happen more often. 'We have gone on marketing during the recession, and people are shopping harder for bargains online,' Paul says. 'In March of 2009 our website got a record number of hits and also of price requests. We opened eleven new stores in the twelve months to July 2009, and start-up sales for those stores have been the best in the company's history. We're doing very well, thanks!

'If we're this busy during a recession, what will it be like when the economy bounces back?' Paul says he's already thinking about how to make the most of the recovery. 'We have invested heavily in our technology and systems. We are now an even more efficient business and well placed to take advantage of growth opportunities as they arise. We're opening quite a few stores to take advantage of cheaper leasing arrangements at the moment. There's no doubt about it—economic downturns throw up opportunities, and you mustn't be afraid to grasp them.'

As for his first million dollars, that's well behind him. 'It was 2003 before we became debt-free, because we invested so much in the business and that required significant borrowing,' Paul says. 'It was a great feeling the first time we turned over $15 million, which was about 2005. But to be honest, we're too busy to think about the money very often. What makes me much happier is the success of the business. In 2007 we won PricewaterhouseCoopers' Franchisor of the Year award, which was a fantastic achievement and made everybody proud. That's the kind of thing that really matters.'

' To be honest, we're too busy to think about the money very often. What makes me much happier is the success of the business. '

So with all that success under his belt, how does Paul reward himself? Fast cars? Champagne every night? A boat, perhaps? 'I love bird watching,' Paul says, 'so I bought myself a pair of $3000 binoculars. That'll do me. I was happy when we had nothing and I'm happy now. I don't see how having more money in the bank is going to make me happier.'

NICK GARDNER

GOLDEN RULES

1. Have an exciting, big, imaginative vision focused on the customer.
2. Avoid negative people. Always stay positive.
3. Work hard and put the hours in—only good can come of it.
4. View your business the way a seasoned long-distance runner views a marathon—focus on endurance rather than speed, and pace yourself to finish strongly.
5. Keep learning. Believe in self-improvement—it is a journey that never stops.
6. Surround yourself with great people who are passionate about the vision.
7. There really are no limits!

Go Green For Gold

Malcolm Rands
EcoStore;
established 1993;
thirty employees;
$8 million turnover

Photo: Sam Ruttyn

Malcolm Rands is not your typical entrepreneur. For one thing, he is a businessman who insists on giving away ten per cent of his profits. For another, he has lived in an environmentally friendly ecovillage. 'It's a community we set up in rural New Zealand with the ethic of trying to work with nature, not fight against it. We wanted to create a permaculture—essentially an agricultural system that copies nature in that it can be left unattended and still be productive. There are jungles in the wild that feed whole communities but are not farmed. I still call it home,' he says.

His other home is in Auckland, from where he oversees the spectacular growth of his company EcoStore, maker of environmentally friendly cleaning products. 'I had to move back to the city to start my international empire,' he jokes. EcoStore products are now on sale in Australia, New Zealand, Hong Kong, the US and the UK, including the Woolworths supermarket chain.

Rands's journey has been a colourful one. He looks back with mixed emotions at his student days, when he was the keyboard player for the Auckland-based band Beaver Shot. He dropped out of university at nineteen to become a full-time musician. He left the band when he concluded that the music business was fickle and he might not have the talent to make it, and set out to travel the world—first stop, Sydney. 'I trained as a radiographer and worked at St Vincent's Hospital for a while before moving on to the US. Travelling was fantastic. It opened my eyes. In California, I fell in with this crowd of rich young kids and we ended up living in a huge house in Orange County, rent free.

'I was living the American dream with people who had more money than sense. Whatever they wanted they could buy. Most people spend their lives trying to get to that state, but I realised then that if you can have everything, your life becomes empty. These people weren't happy. They were trying to fill a gap in their lives with material things. Even then I realised that there's more to life than money, that you have to believe in something.'

So when Rands returned to New Zealand after four years overseas, he turned away from the world of business and profit and tried to follow his passions. He started fund-raising for not-for-profit organisations, then took a job organising community arts festivals in the small town of Whangarei, on the tip of the North Island. 'I had a two-year contract and ended up staying fifteen years,' he recalls. 'I became an expert in business management, fund-raising and events organising. The problem was that you'd spend eleven months slogging it out raising money and only one month doing what you actually loved.'

He and a group of like-minded artists set up the ecovillage in 1987. And it was while living there that he had the brainwave that gave birth to EcoStore. 'We had a nearby water source that produced some of the purest water on the planet.

We thought, Wouldn't it be great if we could make it as clean after we'd used it as it was when it came to us? So we started looking at the way we lived and realised that all the cleaning products we were using in our houses contained the most horrific ingredients, yet we were using that same stuff to water our food gardens. Who knows what that did to the food. This was before there was any requirement to label products or test the ingredients. I thought there must be other people who would want cleaning products that didn't contain such terrible chemicals.'

Rands has always been a realist, and he knew people would not live a green lifestyle if it was too difficult. 'People always think, What difference can I make? I'm just one person, and all that. So I knew I had to make it as easy as possible to go green. That's why cleaning products are such a great area to tackle. It doesn't take any effort at all to buy green cleaning products, yet that kind of everyday action can make a huge difference to the environment.'

The revelation made Rands a capitalist. 'I got a small loan from my brother and started the business in 1993 as a mail-order company, delivering the products to retailers and individuals.'

Four years later, EcoStore had grown into an Auckland-based factory, with its own outlet store, products and research department. 'Fortunately, a supermarket decided to set up next door to us, so all of a sudden we had foot traffic, which made a huge difference to our sales,' says Rands.

The business has continued to boom. Woolworths has expanded its range of EcoStore products from just three to twenty-one. Each product's packet promotes another product in the range, a cost-free promotional technique that helped the company achieve a 40 per cent growth in turnover.

Rands says the downturn has focused consumers' minds on the value of his products. 'We've found that people have ditched more frivolous purchases to continue buying products that are aligned with their personal values. We have also grown in the lower-income demographic. When people analyse how many washes they get from a traditional powder compared to how many they get from ours, they see that our product really does deliver on value.'

Sales have also been boosted by a massive sampling campaign in which the product was given away in supermarkets. 'That really worked wonders. We have to get over the prejudice people have about eco-friendly products: that they're more expensive and not as good. The sampling really helped with that.'

Like other astute businessmen, Rands has seen the downturn as an opportunity to ramp up his marketing, taking advantage of lower costs. He is also trying to squeeze greater economies of scale from his supply chain—but as a matter of good business practice rather than a forced belt-tightening.

From the outset he saw the business as a way of fund-raising for the green cause, and when he found a like-minded partner to invest in the business it was on the understanding that 10 per cent of profits would go to the Fairground Foundation, which supports initiatives to help protect and restore the environment. It was in selling this stake to his sleeping partner that he made his first million. 'I wanted to realise some of the company's worth so my family could enjoy the benefits now rather than later,' he says. 'But it was just as important that I found a partner with similar principles, and I was very lucky in that.

'Sometimes greenies are perceived as having a problem with making money. I don't have any issue with getting rich at all, but I do want to raise funds at the same time.'

'Sometimes greenies are perceived as having a problem with making money,' he adds. 'I don't have any issue with getting rich at all, but I do want to raise funds at the same time.

'The idea for the Fairground Foundation is ultimately to build an urban eco-community that is profitable and sustainable so that others want to copy it. It's easy. You need to make it at least three storeys with a roof garden on the top so everybody has their own outdoor space. Grass is the best roofing material for all sorts of reasons. Then you'd have a tarmac play area and a swimming pool. All these things become cheap to do when you're building a number of apartments.

'For it to work, it would have to have an overriding ethic. It might be that you look after your own grey (waste) water, in which case you could have a wetlands site. If you have a social centre or cinema within the block it enhances the community feeling. This idea has to work with minimal effort from those who live there. If it is hard, or people have to make sacrifices, it won't work.'

Rands says his first urban eco-development will be in Australia or New Zealand. If it's in Sydney, he might end up solving the city's rental shortage as well as cleaning up the world.

NICK GARDNER

GOLDEN RULES

1. Make your profession your passion.
2. Be specific about what you want to achieve.

3. Know your strengths and what you are capable of doing well.
4. Stick to your business principles.
5. Eco-ventures have to produce profits to be sustainable.

The Coffee King Who Changed Australians' Taste

Les Schirato
Cantarella Bros;
established 1947;
150 full-time,
fifty part-time employees;
$160 million turnover

Photo: Angelo Soulas

Only twenty-five years ago Les Schirato was laughed at when he suggested to supermarket chains that they should sell his company's Vittoria brand coffee. Then it was available only in Italian delis, cafés and restaurants, and in the international sections of gourmet food stores. Schirato was advised that Australians would find the coffee too strong. Now Italian staples are everyday items in most Aussie shopping trolleys, and the elegant Schirato is reaping the benefits of his persistence—with a multimillion-dollar business, a Bentley in his garage, a sleek motorboat and a wardrobe of Italian designer suits.

Schirato left school at seventeen to join his father at Cantarella Bros. The aspiring young salesman fell in love with the boss's daughter, Luisa. Realising he would have to prove himself elsewhere if he wanted to marry her, Schirato went to work for Italian car company Fiat. That largely personal decision gave him invaluable professional experience as well as nurturing his love of cars. 'I learned about sales management and people skills,' he says. 'I would be selling trucks one day to a big corporation, and the next day I'd be in Wollongong talking to coal-mine workers. Business is all about relationships. Today, people don't spend the time understanding others. Human relations are important—at every social level.'

As for the relationship with Luisa Cantarella, it flourished. They married in 1983, and Schirato returned to the firm as part of the family. 'I have to be honest, I love what I do. I love to sell coffee and wine and deal with the restaurants and hotels. The money became a fringe benefit.

I never expected the money on the scale it is now; I loved what I did and I had a passion for it. I never sold the business, even though merchant bankers tried to buy us.'

When Schirato came back to Cantarella Bros he launched his push into supermarkets with Vittoria, along with European cheeses, Barilla pasta, Italian mineral water and the then exotic chocolate spread Nutella. Realising that food editors could influence public tastes, Schirato ensured that they received information and ideas on Italian cooking. In an era of chops and three veg, Schirato and his contemporaries helped bring about a food-culture revolution—and make millions for the company in the process.

His father-in-law—whom Schirato bought out, along with his brothers-in-law, in the 1990s—was proud to see Italian foods become such Australian staples. 'He started the company in 1947 when he brought in a roasting machine from Italy,' Schirato says. 'He stuck to strong Italian coffee and he was proud to see how tastes had changed. It's like our coffee beans from all over the world that we mix to make the brand—Australia also takes things from everywhere and blends them together.'

Back then, Cantarella produced Vittoria coffee but was merely a distributor of other products.

Schirato got his next big business lesson when companies for which he'd created an Australian market, such as Barilla, moved in to import and distribute their products themselves. Schirato responded by creating his own products—Aurora Pasta, Santa Vittoria mineral water and Nutino spread—which are made to order in Italy and sold by Cantarella Bros.

This investment, along with Schirato's earlier ambitious push into mainstream markets, took Cantarella from being a $2.5 million company in the early 1980s to one with a turnover of $160 million today. But starting to produce its own brands was a big risk. 'It felt like I was taking the controls of a big plane with all the passengers and shareholders on board. I had their lives in my hands, and I was in the cockpit trying to fly this thing,' he says. 'And, let me tell you, I hate flying.'

'It felt like I was taking the controls of a big plane with all the passengers and shareholders on board. I had their lives in my hands, and I was in the cockpit trying to fly this thing.'

But he learned to do it, and he's landed smoothly. 'We learnt there was no future in building other people's brands,' he says. The average Australian now consumes around 3 kg of pasta a year (a trifling amount compared with Italians' 54 kg) and drink $90 million worth of coffee. Cantarella is the largest Australian vendor of pure coffee.

For Schirato, however, money is not the measure of success. Family remains his cornerstone. His wife, Luisa, is a co-owner of the company, as is his sister-in-law. His son, Rolando, is now marketing manager. 'Find your own balance between work, family, health, community and anything else that's important to you,' he advises. 'Give back every chance you get, and enjoy the journey.'

KERRIE DAVIES

GOLDEN RULES

1. Think like a pilot. Know what your critical gauges are and keep your eyes on these. If they stay green, everything should take care of itself. If you see any flash red, like cash flow, act immediately.
2. Have a flight plan. Give clear directions about where you're going.
3. Look after your profitable customers. First-class passengers are not always the most profitable.
4. Focus on the little things as well as the big things. Pilots have a checklist for a reason. If you miss any of the little things, it could spell disaster.
5. Train your crew. Get involved in key appointments. Give everyone clear, measurable performance indicators and set them up to succeed.

High Flier

Photo: Rohan Kelly

Penny Spencer
Spencer Travel;
established 1998;
twenty-five employees;
$20 million turnover

What's the most lusted-after seat on an aircraft? Penny Spencer knows. 'All my top clients want seat 1A, whether they're famous or not,' she says. 'Particularly on a jumbo jet, because it's right at the front and you're even further forward than the pilots. It's a prestige thing.'

For the upmarket travel agent, flying first class

and staying at luxury hotels is pretty routine. Spencer has an obligation, after all, to sample the high life on behalf of her wealthy clientele. Back in the early 1980s, though, when she got her first job, 'I was so desperate that I literally worked for nothing,' she recalls. 'I worked at a travel agency for six months stamping brochures before they started paying me.' It wasn't quite what Spencer, a New Zealander by birth, had pictured. 'I was fifteen when I got on a plane for the first time,' she says. 'It was only from the South Island to the North, but I knew then that I wanted to work in travel. It was just so exciting.'

A few years of drudgery and a couple of jobs later she was hired by Ursula King Travel, in Sydney's Woollahra, and began six 'inspiring' years of learning from a great mentor. 'Seeing Ursula so passionate about her business, winning awards, even as a woman in a male-dominated world, really made me believe that I could do it too,' Spencer says. 'I learned a lot from her.'

Eventually, after a stint managing an agency with a former colleague, she decided to go it alone. She funded the 1998 launch of Spencer Travel with nothing but credit cards and faith in the loyalty of the clients she had dealt with—and held on to—over the years. 'I still have many of my original clients today,' Spencer says. 'People who appreciate a good service will always stay loyal if they can.'

Her solo venture soon took off, but not without tireless effort and fierce determination. Spencer doggedly pursued a particular TV producer in a bid to win his business. 'I'd heard he wasn't happy with his travel agents, so I called and called and called, and he never answered and didn't return my messages,' she says. 'Then one night I was working late and tried calling his offices in the hope that his secretary wouldn't be there and he'd have to pick up the phone himself. He did. And he said that for my 'sheer perseverance' he'd let me go and see him. Sure enough, he signed me up.' A couple of months later, the same producer won the contract to produce the famous Qantas ad with all the children singing *I Still Call Australia Home*. 'I had to arrange the travel for thirty-six kids and forty crew, parents, guardians, security guards, the lot,' Spencer says. 'They went to five continents and countless locations. I worked solidly for four months. It was exhausting, but I loved it.'

'People who appreciate a good service will always stay loyal if they can.'

That job was the making of Spencer. Word of mouth did the rest. Soon she was employing more people to cope with the demand, especially from the people in the entertainment industry. That was both a blessing and a curse, since they can be fussy travellers.

'We had one very famous and handsome actor who insisted on a ten-man "meet and assist" from the plane through Customs, but it was on a flight to Hong Kong, and the ten-man escort was actually ten giggling, slightly hysterical Chinese air stewardesses,' she says. 'The actor was livid, and insisted nothing like that ever happen again. Unfortunately, the next stop was in Bangkok, where the girls have a similar mentality. So I had to call and persuade the airline to provide either men or girls who wouldn't make a fuss. Then he was annoyed that nobody recognised him.'

A famous and wealthy American woman became so frightened after the September 11 attacks that she refused to use any commercial planes or even commercial airports. 'I had to plan her whole trip from Bermuda to Kuala Lumpur using private jets and military air bases,' Spencer says. 'I pointed out that it would have been cheaper to hire the whole first-class cabin of a Boeing 747 and that it would also mean only one stop, but she insisted she wasn't going to get on a commercial flight. It ended up costing more than $560,000 for that one-way journey.'

It remains the most expensive fare Spencer has ever booked, and that's up against some pretty stiff competition.

Today, she has branched into a new field—the final frontier, even. In 2008 Spencer beat off more than 200 other agents to be chosen by Virgin Galactic as one of nine Australian 'space agents' accredited to sell trips into space. She also became the first agent outside the US to sell a fully paid-for $260,000 ticket. 'It's a three-hour trip into space, and paying upfront ensures that the client will be among the first 100 space tourists once commercial flights begin.' In an industry that has largely done away with travel agents' commissions, Virgin Galactic is making an exception for its space flights (expected to start in 2011). It is paying almost 5 per cent, though Spencer says that it took quite a bit of negotiating.

Spencer is not one of those entrepreneurs who live for work and can never see themselves doing anything else. On the contrary, she started looking for a way to quit in about 2003. 'I've got two very young children, and I want a balance between life and work,' she says. 'I don't want to still be doing this when I'm sixty, so I'll sell up to the staff or to an external buyer.' But if leaving the industry is something she'd readily do for her family, it's not the way she reacts to business downturns. Faced with an obstacle, she simply perseveres and overcomes. There have been many such challenges in recent years. After September 11, 2001, for example, 'Nobody was going anywhere. And there was talk about an end to business travel—that people would start using teleconferencing and virtual meetings. Of course things picked up after a couple of months, but for a while a lot of people in the industry thought it was the end of the road. Then in 2002 there were the Bali bombings and the SARS crisis, and the decision by airlines to stop paying commission to travel agents. They always used to pay us 9 per cent of the cost of the flight, but that was taken away.' Spencer Travel's solution was to charge a service fee. 'That came as a shock, because people weren't used to paying a travel agent. Corporate clients were generally OK about it—they understood that we had to earn a living and charge for a top service. But retail clients were, and still are, harder to persuade. They don't realise that the service fee at other agencies is just bundled up in the price of the ticket.'

Spencer will never forget the first time her firm turned over $1 million in a single month. When that happened, in 2002, 'I was ecstatic,' she says. 'Now I need to hit that mark every month just to break even, but then it was a real milestone.'

The economic downturn has hit her business hard but, far from letting it get her down, she says it has renewed her 'entrepreneurial spirit'. 'In a strange way, there are many positives we've taken from the crisis,' she says. 'It makes you get back to your roots and focus on the basics. I've found I'm thinking with originality again, about how to generate new business and get the numbers back up—just like when I was starting out.

Spencer's old clients are still loyal, but they're flying less and buying cheaper tickets. To make up the lost income, she's looking to new customers and specialising in new areas. Space travel is a big-ticket item but it's yet to take off, so she's focusing her efforts closer to home. 'We've started delivering leaflets in our local area, which is something that we would never have considered before, and we're doing deals with companies to offer prizes as incentives to get people to come to us.'

Spencer is also diversifying into the leisure cruise market. 'I've joined an organisation called Cruiseco, which is basically a bulk buyer of cruise deals and enables us to offer packages at the lowest possible prices.'

She has worked out a plan 'detailing exactly how much we have to make each month and what needs to be done if we don't meet those targets. I have stuck to that, and it's meant considerable changes.' Over Christmas 2008 Spencer put her employees on four-day weeks, and from March to June 2009 they worked nine-day fortnights. 'My staff understood,' she says. 'They would rather be working shorter weeks than be out of a job.' They are back to full-time now.

And she's far from pessimistic about the future. 'The economy might be struggling, but people still need to travel—and when the economy does rebound, our leaner, meaner and more innovative structure means we should be well placed to benefit.' Oh, and those plans to leave the business are still on hold.

NICK GARDNER

GOLDEN RULES

1. Know your financial situation on a daily basis.
2. Be passionate—you have to enjoy what you do.
3. Don't be afraid of making difficult decisions in tough times.
4. Be flexible and always open to new ideas and changes in direction.
5. Be positive—if you aren't, your staff will not feel optimistic either.
6. Cash is king—keep as much as you can.

He Chose To Kick Goals

Photo: Carlos Furtado

Peter Switzer
Switzer Group;
established 2005;
twenty-three employees;
$4 million-plus turnover

As a nifty prop with a desire to wear an Easts' rugby league jersey, Peter Switzer was faced with a momentous decision when the curtain fell on his teenage years. He could chase a sporting career he knew was well within his reach, or hit the books and get a degree. For his business-minded father the choice was clear. But for the young Switzer it was an agonising dilemma. The league life wasn't his only sporting option, either: he played first-grade water polo and won a Sydney title in the early 1970s with North Bondi Surf Club. 'I had a choice: President's Cup or a Master of Commerce. Thankfully I chose the latter,' he says.

Thankful is probably an understatement clothed in humility, given the accolades Switzer has garnered as one of Australia's leading business commentators and advocates. His brand and his pedestal is Switzer Financial Services, which he founded under the motto of 'trusted provider of accounting, business and financial advice'. But he admits that it wasn't his own business that propelled him into the millionaires' realm but some smart property purchases in the 1970s.

Raising a young family, Switzer and his wife Maureen didn't have much cash to spare. 'We moved into Paddington in 1979, when it was not a trendy suburb,' says Switzer. 'I recall my father-in-law seeing our purchase—an old Victorian cottage—and saying: "Oh, love! Sell this as quickly as you can." But the home launched our interest in real estate. We bought old homes in great suburbs and renovated them. Your principal property is capital gains tax-free when you sell it, and that makes it a great way to build wealth.'

After completing his Master of Commerce, Switzer worked as a teacher at several private schools before moving on to the economics faculty of the University of New South Wales and starting his first business, an economics coaching school. After thirteen years in academe he was, as he puts it, seduced away by Radio Triple M's then ratings-leading breakfast radio host, Doug Mulray.

As he expanded from radio spots on finance into TV and newspaper columns, Switzer transformed his coaching school into a media company. On the side, he and Maureen also created a publishing firm which at first they ran from their Paddington home, all while raising their young family.

The rewards for those years of toil took a while to show. 'We added financial planning and business coaching to our media and publishing business because there are great synergies,' Switzer says. 'After years of writing about personal investment, we decided to create a financial planning business that upholds the highest standards of honesty and transparency. That gave us a competitive edge. As a natural progression we created Switzer Business Coaching, which teaches principles I have been taught and admire. So our business is now about providing business information, education and advice to media organisations, corporations, small businesses, investors and consumers.'

Though his array of roles keeps him busy, Switzer has maintained his love affair with real estate. It is about diversifying his financial portfolio, he explains—something he frequently instructs clients to do. 'Most people are amateurs when it comes to investment and wealth building. I hate people treating investment like punting,' Switzer says. 'Day traders can be on the spot and, if they are smart, make more good decisions than bad ones. But a lot don't. I tell my clients and readers that we're in for the long run. We buy great blue-chip assets, especially when they are well priced, and we hold on to them. It works for all asset classes and brings good returns.'

> 'Most people are amateurs when it comes to investment and wealth building. I hate people treating investment like punting.'

But Switzer never wants the enterprise to depend on him alone. His sons Martin and Alex also work in the business, a source of solidarity and support that Switzer finds especially valuable in difficult economic times.

For Switzer, the chief benefit of wealth is that it expands one's choices. 'The funny thing is I could retire and relax, but I love writing, building our business, educating Australians and helping our clients to create wealth and great businesses,' he says. 'I always say you should do something that you are absolutely passionate about, which means you can play to your strengths. And don't be afraid to seek expert help to get the best out of yourself.'

Once, after Switzer had given a speech on the importance of business coaching, he was approached by a woman who asked if he had had any business coaching himself. When he said no, she quoted him saying moments earlier that we all need someone else's objective eyes to get the best out of us. Undone by her quiet reasoning, Switzer took the woman up on her offer of three months' free business coaching. Now she is a Switzer Group business coaching partner.

After the financial crisis Switzer's firm has received fewer inquiries about business coaching, but the people who make them are much more likely to follow through and enrol. 'They can see it is a false economy not to invest in improving themselves, especially in such uncertain times,' he says.

The financial planning division has held up well, in part because Switzer has always charged a flat fee rather than a percentage-based one. As fund values have fallen, percentage fees have too.

But Switzer has been in great demand for

speaking engagements and on television and radio. He now has an eponymous slot on Sky Business four nights a week, interviewing experts about investing and economic forecasting.

Switzer is advising his business coaching clients to go back to basics and devote themselves to making sure their best customers are happy. 'Show your customers consideration and it generates great loyalty,' he says. 'One great salesman I know sends his clients little newspaper links or cuttings if he thinks they might prove useful. That's a terrific idea. It shows real concern. Another good piece of advice is to network more. Turn up to more events, and don't go anywhere without business cards. And when you are at an event, have a quick script in your head to let you succinctly explain your business. That could generate work for you straight away.'

Finally, Switzer says, analyse your marketing to see if it's doing all you need it to. 'Use the purple cow principle,' he says. 'The American marketeer Seth Godin says our marketing messages can be like black-and-white cows in a field—all looking the same. But imagine if the farmer painted a cow purple. People would all point and say, Look at the purple cow!'

With marketing like that, the sky is the limit.

ANDREW CARSWELL

GOLDEN RULES

1. Market like never before.
2. Make sure cash flow is fantastic.
3. Make sure you communicate with staff to engage them.
4. Make sure the vision of your business is understood by everybody in the business—and don't be afraid to tell customers about the need for feedback.

That Aussie Bloke

John Symond
Aussie Home Loans;

established 1992; 1000 employees; about $1 billion worth of home loan applications each month

Photo: Andy Baker

Considering the infamous indulgences of his $50 million Point Piper pad, one enters the city office of 'Aussie' John Symond expecting big things. Surely there'll be a basketball-court-sized desk, hewn from the salvaged deck of the *Endeavour*, a wall-sized plasma screen and a ceiling plastered with $100 bills. In fact, the décor is more functional than flashy, and the occupant a self-confessed workaholic who says his mind is so hyperactive he gets barely four hours of fitful sleep a night.

Sitting in his office, Symond could be any chief executive except when he discusses money. A one-time debt of $5 million is mentioned with a dismissive flick of the wrist that suggests the sum is a mere trifle. Given that Symond's now worth more than $500 million, it is. As for his first million dollars, he has trouble recalling precisely when he passed that minor milestone. 'I was a young articled clerk for a law firm, but at the same time I was learning the ropes about property from my uncle and father. I bought and sold properties and would have made my first million when I was in my late twenties,' Symond says. 'That was a lot of money back then. I invested it back in real estate. But I lost most of that first million on property, too. I remember investing in building some units and there was a recession. But you learn from your mistakes.'

Symond's biggest ever error was entering a joint venture with the State Bank of South Australia. 'It was the late 1980s, when interest rates were hitting 20 per cent. I just never thought, being naïve, that a government-owned bank could go belly up,' he recalls. The memory clearly still riles him. That experience fired a dislike of the major banks that would inspire Symond in 1992 to set up Aussie Home Loans, which changed the way money was lent in this country. With his 'arse on fire', creditors at the door and bankruptcy looming, Symond decided to fight back. 'It was just total devastation,' he says. 'My greatest motivation was having a three-year-old and a seven-year-old and not wanting them to be denied an education. I hated the thought of them saying: "Oh, yeah, my dad went bankrupt." So that wasn't an option.

'And I was so incensed by the way the banks, the big banks, were treating thousands upon thousands of Australians who had got themselves in strife through no real fault of their own. So I worked out a deal with my creditors, giving me three years to pay back about $5 million.' An ordinary salary clearly wasn't going to be large enough to make those payments, so Symond set up his own financial institution, undercut the big banks, filmed some now notorious ads and made a fortune. 'People say, "Why did you do your own ads?" Well, at the time I

'My greatest motivation was having a three-year-old and a seven-year-old and not wanting them to be denied an education.'

couldn't afford to hire any real talent,' Symond explains. 'It taught me the importance of marketing yourself, because people will listen to you.'

In 2008, Symond sold 33 per cent of Aussie to Commonwealth Bank and used funding from the bank to buy rival Wizard Home Loans. That development was as much of a surprise to him as it was to everybody else. 'If you had said to me a year ago that I'd have appointed a CEO to take on the day-to-day running of the business and gone into a partnership with a big bank, I'd have said, "What are you smoking, mate? You must be mad!" But I learned a long time ago that the best way of predicting the future is to create it—and that means being proactive and not being afraid to change.'

> 'People say, "Why did you do your own ads?" Well, at the time I couldn't afford to hire any real talent.'

Symond's face, and voice, on those ads helped him establish a bond of trust with the public, he believes: 'I can't walk fifty paces without people walking up and asking for advice, and they feel very comfortable in doing that,' he says. 'And I always stop and talk, whether it's the garbo or the policeman or whoever.' Symond believes his working-class roots are the key to his everyman appeal, and he gives his parents—who owned fruit shops where he worked as a boy—much of the credit for his success. 'My greatest role models were my mum and dad. They didn't have a lot of formal education, but I learned more from them than I did from eleven schools and two universities,' he says.

'I thank my lucky stars that I grew up working class because it means that I can relate well to mums and dads in suburbia. If you're born into a privileged situation, you really don't know what makes people tick.'

While the long property boom filled his coffers, Symond says he's appalled by house prices. 'Houses are just too expensive, and the dream of home ownership is becoming a nightmare for many people. Governments are milking the golden goose dry with all their various taxes, and the way we're going it's not going to be possible for younger people to own their own homes. That will have serious consequences for our economy,' Symond warns.

Money isn't a panacea, he says, 'but it does help when you're going shopping'. He likes to spend his spare cash on boats, cars, watches, contemporary Australian art and his spectacular house that overlooks the Sydney Opera House, the largest private residence in Australia. 'I do like to shop. My staff know not to let me have any spare time because if I do, I'll go and buy a watch or something. I really like watches,' he says.

> 'My greatest role models were my mum and dad. They didn't have a lot of formal education, but I learned more from them than I did from eleven schools and two universities.'

And all the time his mind is racing. 'It's very hard for me to just relax and turn off, but I find being on the water, whether in a dinghy or a bigger boat, really helps. And I'm lucky, because I've got a nice boat and a beautiful home on the water. Every day I pinch myself and think how very fortunate I've been.'

But he also feels he's achieved something worthwhile. Looking back, 'The big breakthrough was when, after we'd been undercutting the big banks for a while, they turned around and dropped their home-loan interest rates by almost 3 per cent,' he says. 'I know that put money in the pockets of millions of Australians. And that makes me proud.'

STEPHEN CORBY

GOLDEN RULES

1. You must look after your staff. I've always believed that your No. 1 customers are the

people who work with you. If they don't trust you, if they don't believe in you, they're not going to be loyal to you.

2. Show strong leadership, and people will follow you.
3. Concentrate on your core business and cut out all unnecessary expenses.
4. Don't be afraid of partnerships if they're necessary.
5. Talk to positive, successful people and ask them how they got there.
6. Learn from your mistakes and embrace change. And be brave. There are opportunities even in recessions.

Special Blend For Success

Photo: Anthony Reginato

Angela Vithoulkas

VIVO Group;

established 2003;
twenty-eight employees;
$2 million-plus turnover

Angela Vithoulkas was born into the cafe business: her mother's waters broke at the family's suburban milk-bar cafe as she was making coffee. By the age of three she had caught her first shoplifters: she ran after boys stealing lollies and smacked them with a broom.

When Vithoulkas was seventeen, in 1983, she and her older brother, Con, started their own cafe in William Street, Sydney. They sold it at a 100 per cent profit two years later: 90 per cent of cafes fail within five years. Vithoulkas and her brother now own Vivo Cafes—three sites on George Street, in the city centre—which turn over $3 million a year. 'People think of cafes as small business, but it's anything but small,' Vithoulkas says. 'We are setting a new standard for small business. My mother is very proud of us, but she can't understand why we keep taking risks opening new businesses. But we love what we do. It's not about the money—it's about the adventure.'

Vithoulkas's mother would dearly like to see her successful daughter married to one of those nice city suits who frequent the cafes. Although whoever wants to date her must accept her tremendous work ethic, which sees her rise at 4 a.m. most weekdays to prepare for the morning rush and power on till 8 p.m. or later. In 2007 Vithoulkas won the Telstra NSW Business Women's award. She and Con had already won City of Sydney Business Awards for Business of the Year in 2006 and outstanding cafe of the year in 2005 and 2006.

From her first few months in that first cafe, Angelique's, Vithoulkas has been learning continuously. Her parents put up half the money for that business, but it was up to Angela and Con to make it work. Within three months, however, they faced disaster when Con nearly died in an accident that killed other family members. Vithoulkas was left alone in the business while Con spent months in hospital. 'After his accident, my employees demanded that I pay them double or they'd leave,' Vithoulkas recalls.

It was a painful trial for a teenager who had never worked with anyone but family. 'It's horrible to fire someone. You don't often plan that, so you don't have a replacement. But I thought I'd rather close the business than be blackmailed like that.'

Vithoulkas struggled on alone until Con was well enough to join her and they have worked together ever since, splitting responsibilities according to their talents. She's good at people management, so she handles staff, customers and suppliers; he has a knack for efficiency, streamlining procedures and spending. For more than twenty years now they have bought failing cafes and transformed them into buzzing venues supplying successful corporate catering. But it's a slow-burn money-maker: the real profit doesn't come until they sell the business.

Angela and Con's third venture turned a near-broke cafe into one of Sydney city's first

European-style, al-fresco havens. They added 200 seats and introduced paper cups instead of polystyrene so the coffee tasted better. The sale of that business after five years brought them their first million dollars. 'Taking over businesses that have a history of failure is an enormous risk and a stressful road full of obstacles. There are absolutely no guarantees—except that it probably won't work,' Vithoulkas says.

'Why do we do it? We don't dwell too much on this, except to say that it's what we do—start with what looks like a disaster, pull it apart, reorganise it, turn it into a challenge and then conquer it.'

During the 2001 stock market crash they lost most of their fortune. 'It was very difficult to lose that amount of money,' Vithoulkas admits. They sank the remainder into the original Vivo cafe in 2003 and have now regained what they lost. 'It's always hard to find a good site,' Vithoulkas says. 'Despite its position, this business was bankrupt. The rent hadn't been paid in two years. When we bought it, all the money went into back rent and paying the suppliers.' Why did they succeed where others had failed? 'We knew the cafe business. Running a small business is tough—it's always tough. You are opening a door without any customers, continuously funding it and wondering whether you can pay anyone, including yourself.'

Knowing the customer, especially the city office-worker breed, has been crucial to their success and, more recently, their very survival. Thousands of their customers were made redundant as the financial crisis hit the big end of town. But Vithoulkas saw the writing on the wall and acted fast. 'It wasn't difficult to see what was coming. We are in the central business district, and when one building loses 700 people—and these people represent your customer base—you can lose your business in a heartbeat. If you lose 20 per cent of your turnover, where do you go?

> 'Why do we do it? We don't dwell too much on this, except to say that it's what we do—start with what looks like a disaster, pull it apart, reorganise it, turn it into a challenge and then conquer it.'

'I knew that not only did we have to retain as many customers as possible, we had to find new ones, because so many of our existing ones were clearly going to vanish.' So Vithoulkas got busy planning. Store renovations, new menus, new prices and a fresh attitude from the staff all played their part in transforming the business. 'The crisis has hit workers from all walks of life—everybody is more money-conscious now, so we had to offer better value and focus on service. Consumers are savvy, and you cannot take their loyalty for granted. I asked myself what we were doing well, in every part of the business, and then figured out a way of doing it better for less. Now the company is in the best shape it's ever been. When the recovery comes, we will be very well positioned.'

Today, the company is turning over around 30 per cent more than before the crisis—an extraordinary achievement.

Vithoulkas has noticed over the past few years that the pace of working life has sped up dramatically: 'The days of the long lunch are over,' she says. 'People are meeting for a coffee now—to save time as well as money.'

All leftover food from Vivo Cafes is given to OzHarvest to feed the homeless. Vithoulkas also supports the Nelune Foundation, which helps people with cancer buy special food that assists their diet during chemotherapy. Vithoulkas became involved through a customer. 'We do get to know people here,' she says.

She and Con are now planning to franchise Vivo, but they hope to keep it more personal than international chains such as Starbucks. 'We want to conquer the world,' Vithoulkas says. 'One coffee at a time.'

KERRIE DAVIES

GOLDEN RULES

1. Attitude is everything. Be positive and brave.
2. Don't be afraid to admit you have been making mistakes and to put them right.
3. Be prepared to spend money on innovations, regardless of economic conditions.
4. Everything is negotiable except your vision.
5. There is nothing wrong with Plan B.